JUST ANOTHER TIN FOIL HAT PRESENTS

ZELIA EDGAR

BEYOND THE FRAY
Publishing

BEYOND THE FRAY

Publishing

This book is dedicated to my mom.
Thank you for raising me with curiosity as a core value and love an unwavering force.

CONTENTS

ACKNOWLEDGMENTS

First of all, I would like to thank Chad Lewis for the fantastic foreword, as well as for the dedication and expertise he brings to this field of research. His guidance has served as a veritable roadmap in my pursuit of the unknown.

Also, a thank you to Linda Godfrey. Along with Chad, these two Wisconsin researchers served as true inspiration to a young girl with an interest in the unexplained; my life would be very different without their influence.

Much appreciation is due to the researchers who have graciously shared their time and information with me, namely Joshua Cutchin, Todd Roll and Matt Thomas.

A special thanks to my 'fellow parishioner at the Church of John Keel', Steve Ward, whose friendship and encouragement have been invaluable.

Finally, a thank you to my family, especially Mom, my sisters Lily and Chloe, Grandma, my aunts Diane and Joan, and my cousins Maryam and Aaron, who all lived through an eleven-year-old cryptozoologist's insistence that Bigfoot really could be anywhere, including Dubuque's Eagle Point Park. Much love to you all.

FOREWORD

BY CHAD LEWIS

Zelia Edgar is exactly the type of researcher that this field desperately needs right now. In today's world, the internet is brimming with reports of the strange and unusual, yet the overwhelming majority of these postings consist of nothing more than a scary headline or snippet of information designed to get as many clicks as possible. Dozens of websites post hundreds of daily stories with no deep investigative dive, no in-depth contemplation, and no follow-up research. Eventually this parade of nonstop witness reports fades into the background as the stories morph into nothing more than supernatural white noise.

This bizarre new world consisting of only cursory internet searching is precisely what makes Zelia's weighty research so vital. She is skillfully following in the investigative footsteps of John Keel, Rosemary Ellen Guiley, Jacques Vallee, and Jerome Clark. Zelia smartly takes a step back and ponders the ramifications of these legends and experiences. She devotes the significant time and energy necessary to formulate theories to help explain any possible deeper meaning or connections that may be linking many of these phenomena together. More importantly, Zelia is on a quest to understand the direct impact that folklore has on us, both on a personal level and in the greater cultural context.

I first met Zelia about a decade and a half ago when her mother, Lori, arrived with Zelia and her sisters in tow at one of my presentations on the supernatural. At the time Zelia was an eleven-year-old paranormal enthusiast who seemed hell-bent on exploring all topics of the supernatural. When the program ended, we chatted about some paranormal topics that I can no longer recall – probably some sea serpent sightings or haunted legends from the area. We continued to talk as Zelia and her wonderful family began attending more of my lectures. Even at that young age it was evident to me that Zelia approached the field of the strange and unusual in a different manner than most preteen kids. As the years passed, I began to notice that the manner in which Zelia analyzed cases was on a much higher and broader level than most researchers. Her insightful observations and unique perspective began to mold her into a researcher that was considerably different than what was currently being offered.

The book you hold in your hands serves as the fantastic fruits of all Zelia's painstaking labor. I feel that reading this book is just like seeing your favorite band perform live. Of course, the band is going to play their greatest hits, (the

Flatwoods Monster, the Hopkinsville Hobgoblins), the iconic songs that everyone in the audience knows and loves, yet being that it is a live performance, the songs will suddenly sound differently from how you have previously heard them – they will be more heartfelt, energetic, and speak to you in beautiful new ways. The band will also carefully sprinkle in some of their more obscure tunes (the Case of the Cussac Devils, the Three-Ring Circus of Cisco Grove), great songs that many people might not be as familiar with. In short order this new group of songs will inevitably be thrust into the category with your old favorites. As the concert progresses, you will start to appreciate the expert manner in which the playlist was constructed, and by the end of the show, the entire crowd has a whole new appreciation of the band's work. When you finish this book, you will undoubtedly want to purchase the band's T-shirt – or maybe a "Just Another Tin Foil Hat" one instead.

My absolute favorite thing about this book is how it effortlessly transported me back to my early days when I was just starting out in this field. I can still vividly recall when Jerome Clark's 1993 book *Unexplained!* was released. I absolutely adored how I could read about living dinosaurs in one chapter and strange falls from the sky in the next. The sheer variety of weirdness was intoxicating. When I began reading Zelia's book, that same excited feeling of adventure and wonderment came flooding back to me as I read about strange space leprechauns one night, and a puzzling hairy humanoid creature the next. I have already cleared off a spot in my bookcase next to Jerome Clark's *Unexplained!* book where I can proudly put this one – as both have served as an emotionally significant reminder of why I love this field of research so deeply.

I have absolutely no doubt that you are going to thoroughly enjoy Zelia's bizarre journey down the backroads of the supernatural as much as I have. As you finish the last page and your reading adventure with this book unfortunately comes to its unavoidable end – when you take stock of what this book has ignited in you – I wonder what title you will choose to place it next to on your bookshelf.

Keep an eye out,

Chad Lewis
Researcher of the weird and unusual

INTRODUCTION

What do a chicken farmer, a serial killer, and an interior decorator have in common? No, there's no punchline here. Just the fact that these three individuals – Joe Simonton, Darrell Rich, and Millard Faber, respectively – each had their own brush with the unexplained. And not just your run-of-the-mill weirdness. Intense weirdness or – to use as close to a respectable term as such events can lay claim to – high strangeness.

In Simonton's case, it was a trio of pancake-slinging, turtleneck-wearing flying saucer occupants. Rich, later to become known as the Hilltop Rapist, was just a teen when he and three friends witnessed a bumpy, 'pouch-covered' entity and, fleeing the scene, were barraged by light anomalies. Faber's sighting of Sasquatch outside Sandusky, Ohio, was considered 'the by-now standard Sasquatch or Bigfoot report' – until, less than a week after the incident, he was visited by five spectral, glowing humanoids in his bedroom.

We are in the boondocks of the Twilight Zone, a place where half-formed concepts cavort with full-fledged nightmares. There are no clear boundaries here. Occurrences and appearances bleed through the tidy, self-contained categories that convention dictates should stand. Patterns exist between all anomalies, whether they be cryptid encounters, hauntings, UFO sightings, poltergeist phenomena, religious apparitions, folkloric beliefs, or demonic manifestations. The evidence at once points two separate ways – to physical occurrences that can't solely abide by physical laws. Objective events that revel in subjective appearances. Simply put, the evidence points to something paradoxical.

I started my YouTube channel as an outlet for my greatest lifelong interest – paranormal research. This book is a compendium of cases that I've covered in these first several years, and naturally the question arises: why these accounts in particular? Whether obscure, such as the Walking Tree Stumps or the Flight-suit Entity, or well-known, like Momo or the Flatwoods Monster, each case embodies some of the strangest occurrences the unknown has to offer.

A word of warning – to quote Thomas Jerome Newton, the extraterrestrial from Walter Tevis's fantastic novel *The Man Who Fell to Earth*, "I'm not a scientist." And I'm certainly not. I'm simply someone who has been interested in this sort of thing for a long time, gathering information from a wide variety of different sources, belief systems, and cultures. This is a work of speculative nonfiction; I have taken the strangest of strange cases and sifted through them in an attempt to uncover some deeper truth about the unexplained, about us, and about the possible relation between the two.

Finally, a note on taxonomy – throughout this book, there are terms such as UFO, flying saucer, robot, humanoid, monster, devil, etc. In the spirit of full disclosure, when handling these anomalies, I choose to use the terms used by the witness, in the vernacular of their beliefs. While it is my conviction that the truth regarding all of these entities is likely far stranger than the hardwired concepts these terms imply, it is also my belief that it is crucial to catalogue every angle of the witness's encounter as they perceived and believed it, as it is these perceptions and beliefs we are able to study.

CASE 1

THAT STRANGE NIGHT

Growing up, I was fortunate enough to spend a lot of time at my grandma's house in Platteville, Wisconsin. Firmly nestled in the Driftless Area, a geological oddity so named due to its lack of the glacial deposits, or drift, of the last ice age, Platteville is an old, folk-storied town that first made its living as a gateway to the subterranean world of lead mines. Its survival past the mining boom of the late 1800s was in large part due to its focus on academia, including the establishment of Wisconsin's first teachers college in 1866.

The pride of Platteville is undoubtably the Platte Mound M, known locally as "the Big M". Perched on the side of the Platte Mound, the highest point in Lafayette County, the M is crafted out of whitewashed limestone and stands 241 feet tall. It maintains the title as the largest hillside "M" in the world. Although my uncle told me it stood for his first name, Mike, while my mom said that, obviously, it stood for Mom, the "M" stands for "Miners".

However, the M is not the only landmark of note on the Platte Mound. Back away from the road, which snakes its way around the mound, is a dilapidated two-story stone house, the hollow remains of the Nodolf family home. This was the setting of one of the stories I grew up with – the Nodolf Incident or, as it is still known around Platteville, "That Strange Night".

SOMETIME IN THE 1880S, a farmer by the name of Carl Nodolf occupied that house with his wife, Louise, and their two children, Minnie Louise and Louie. At the time of their anomalous experience, Minnie was four and Louie was two. One summer night, a massive storm ravaged the mound. Carl and Louise waited it out for some time, then decided to turn in for the night as the storm continued wailing outside. The storm wasn't the only disturbance that night; Louise also wondered at the howling of wolves, which, although a common enough noise, seemed closer to the cozy stone house than usual.

After barring the doors and shuttering the windows, Carl and Louise checked on the children. They found them safely tucked in their beds, and so retired for the evening themselves.

Close to morning, a massive thunderclap awakened the two parents. Louise heard the children crying for her and went to comfort them. What she found is any parent's worst nightmare; both of the youngsters were gone.

At this point in time, Louise and Carl believed that the kids must have simply gone downstairs, frightened by the storm. However, when they checked the first story, the children were nowhere to be found. Still, they heard their cries and gradually realized that they were coming from outside the home.

However, the doors and windows were still bolted and shuttered from inside. What's more, the children weren't even tall enough to reach the bolts to undo them. This probably wasn't the first priority at the moment, as Louise and Carl ran outside and found their children out in the driving rain. They quickly carried them inside, then ran to get dry clothes.

To make matters even stranger, both the children were bone-dry, while their parents had gotten drenched just walking through the storm. When questioned, Minnie and Louie couldn't say what had happened to them, as they had developed a terrible stutter.

Local legends maintained that both the children would stutter from then on out. However, the daughter of Minnie Louise, Mrs. Gordon Williams, would later rebuff that claim in a letter to the editor of the *Platteville Journal*. This clipping was provided to me by UW Platteville's Karmann Library director, historian and folklorist Todd Roll, and states that Minnie Louise "was certainly able to speak", and grew up to "marry and rear a family of six". As for the rest of the tale, there never was a definitive answer as to how the children had gotten outside the locked home or stayed dry in the torrential rain.

According to Gard and Soren's classic tome *Wisconsin Lore*, legends dictate that the families near the mound had been especially worried about the Nodolf family that night, as it seemed to them that the storm had settled right over the Nodolfs' farm.

This account is a mainstay of Southwestern Wisconsin folklore and has haunted me ever since hearing it from my grandma when I was very young. In her telling of the tale, she claimed that the rapping of a poltergeist could be heard in the home from then on. According to another clipping from the *Platteville Journal* provided to me by Todd Roll, "House Haunted in 1830s Still Stands Near Mound", from that night onward, there was a "stumping on the stairs" each morning around three o'clock.

The article dictates that the local populace believed the disturbances to be due to ghosts.

A TIE to the dominant theme of displacement can be found in another folktale of the area; a mere twelve miles away from the Platte Mound is the town of Annaton, which, according to *Driftless Spirits: Ghosts of Southwest Wisconsin* by Dennis Boyer, disappears and reappears from time to time. Unfortunately – or fortunately – for me, every time I've checked, Annaton is safe and sound.

Later fans of the unexplained have made connections

between this case and later accounts of alien abduction, or even the mystifying Missing 411 phenomenon researched by David Paulides. Paulides's research details odd and unexplained disappearances of people, including young children. Important here is the fact that, of the missing individuals who are located, there is usually a lapse of memory regarding what transpired while they were away, including how they arrived at some different location.

At the end of the day, the displacement of the children most calls to mind cases of "apport", or the spiritualist belief that objects can simply be transported from point A to point B with no travel in between. Regarding people, it's usually referred to as transportation. The fact that the home was later host to continual knocks at the same time each night definitely calls to mind manifestations typically associated with poltergeist phenomena, which can, in some cases, include apport of objects or transportation of people.

Too, the folklore of this area is dominated by the beliefs carried over by the Cornish – it is, in fact, the "Cornish-men" that the *Platteville Journal* referenced as believing ghosts were responsible for the children's temporary vanishing act. The Cornish brought over other beliefs as well; one of the most popular is that of the tommyknockers, mine spirits near and dear to their chief business of lead mining.

However, it is a different Cornish entity that is of particular interest in this case: the "pisky", better known by its nonlocalized name, "pixie". As catalogued in Evans-Wentz's *The Fairy-Faith in Celtic Countries*, the Cornish pisky was believed to go about the same business as many other types of fairies, particularly the abduction or exchanging of children. Of interest, regarding the thought that the Nodolf house was "haunted", is the Cornish belief that related the piskies to spirits of the dead, a belief also common across the British Isles regarding other types of fairies.

Am I suggesting that "the Good Folk", as fairies of all sorts were euphemistically referred to, were responsible for the displacement of Minnie and Louie that stormy night in the 1880s? Or perhaps that a ghost spirited them outside for reasons unknown? Or that the beliefs of that time fell short in understanding the truth – that a posse of extraterrestrials scooped them up in a classic alien abduction, returning them – not to their beds, but outside the home?

None of the above, as it turns out. A recurring theme of this book, and my research at large, has to do with the notion that beliefs regarding the paranormal are simply that, beliefs, and that, as of yet, an explanation for these varied disturbances remains, as in the case of the Nodolf incident, unknown.

CASE 2

THE FLATWOODS MONSTER

Few paranormal accounts have captured the public imagination as much as the Braxton County Monster – better known as the Flatwoods Monster. This gliding monstrosity with its spade-topped silhouette is an icon of the unexplained, towering over the fields of ufology and cryptozoology in particular. This pop-culture fervor has been a driving force for the evolving image of the creature whose infamous tale has graced the pages of numerous books, countless T-shirts, and even *The Legend of Zelda* game series' creepiest incarnation, *Majora's Mask*.

THE STORY BEGINS the evening of September 12, 1952. A group of boys, which included twelve-year-old Fred May and his thirteen-year-old brother Edward, were playing football at the Flatwoods School Playground. A little after seven o'clock, they saw a glowing, red, vaguely pear-shaped object come around a nearby hill, stop, and then appear to descend on a nearby property.

The group soon decided they wanted to see where this strange sight had ended up, and so a small posse formed from the group of boys. It included the two May children, fourteen-year-old Neal Nunley, and three ten-year-old boys: Tommy Hyer, Teddie Neal, and Ronald Shaver. According to Ivan Sanderson's investigations, Neal Nunley's primary purpose for going to look was because he believed the strange sight to be a meteorite and wanted to collect any pieces that may have survived its fall to Earth. Along the way, they ran past the May household, where Fred and Eddie's mother, Kathleen May, asked where they were off to.

Reportedly, Ronald Shaver replied that they were going to look for a crashed flying saucer. However, at the time, he was alone in this conviction.

Kathleen then asked a visiting neighbor, seventeen-year-old National Guardsman Eugene Lemon, to accompany them all with his flashlight. The posse was also joined by Lemon's dog.

As they neared the area, they became aware that the spot around the object's landing site was marked by a red-purple glow. As they approached it, they noticed a warm mist, accompanied by a sickening, sulfuric odor that burned their eyes and noses. Lemon's dog stopped, then ran growling into the mist. They could hear it barking until, after a few minutes, it ran back to town, tail between its legs. Most reports of this incident state that it died two days later after experiencing continual, intense vomiting, but according to a later interview with the May brothers in Small Town Monsters' documentary *The Flatwoods Monster: A Legacy of Fear*, the dog thankfully survived.

When questioned about the object later, the boys would all agree that it was visible there on the hillside, claiming that it was about the size of a particular outhouse located on the May property, and that it was pointed on top. At this point in time, they also claimed that it was black – though Ronald Shaver would note that it appeared as if it was becoming red hot.

As they traversed the last bend before the "landing site", Kathleen called out that she saw the eyes of a possum or raccoon up in a tree. Neal turned his flashlight in that direction, and needless to say, the beam didn't rest upon a friendly neighborhood garbage gourmand.

Instead, what the group saw was something described

by Kathleen across multiple articles as looking "worse than Frankenstein".

The first detail, agreed upon by all the witnesses, was that the entity was absolutely metallic in nature. Hovering some feet off the ground, the actual height of the being was only around six feet tall. Its silhouette was dominated by the now iconic pointed, "ace of spades"-shaped collar or hood. In front of this was a bright red, helmetlike head. The torso was cylindrical and flared from the waist in something akin to a metallic, pleated skirt; with the exception of the head, the rest of the body was a bright green. The key witnesses did not note the by now infamous claw-like arms, which appear to be an artifact of later artistic renderings. The transition from a robotic, metallic-like entity to the more classic, midcentury monster image known so well today occurred through the many renderings of the creature in news programs, even coining the then-popular moniker "the Green Monster".

The "eyes" of the creature appeared like orbs of light behind a translucent panel, or "porthole", and projected strong, flashlight-like beams. At first, these beams of light were directed up in the air in a southerly direction, but as soon as Eugene's flashlight beam hit this monstrosity, it turned to face the frightened party of witnesses. Then, to the posse's horror, it began gliding towards them, all the while emitting more of the strange mist and shrill hisses. Eugene Lemon had had enough at this point and fell into a dead faint. Thankfully, the others didn't leave him to the mist and the monster but grabbed him up and tore back into town.

The trouble was far from over. Everyone who had come into close proximity with the creature began experiencing symptoms categorized by a local doctor as similar to those caused by mustard gas, including intense nausea and vomiting.

Upon returning to the May household, they contacted other adults, who formed an impromptu, gun-toting posse. A brief search of the hill revealed nothing, though Nunley was under the impression that the search was anything but thorough. When reporters scoured the site about three hours later, the sickening odor was still present, and there were two six-to-eight-foot-diameter circles of trampled brush.

Mrs. May would later return to the area and found oily skid marks about a car and a half in length.

However, the infamous sighting of the Flatwoods Monster was not the only strange occurrence at the time. As catalogued in Ivan T. Sanderson's *Uninvited Visitors*, multiple sightings of strange, luminous objects in the sky were observed that very night. Mr. Woodrow Eagle had even called the sheriff regarding what he believed was a plane crash on a hill near Sugar Creek; he had observed a flaming object descend into the nearby woods. A man living nearby confirmed that he had indeed seen a "meteor", which came horizontally across the sky, turned, and then descended into the same area described by Eagle.

SOME OF THE most intriguing aspects of this case have to do with cultural response. One of these responses was the eventual transition of the Flatwoods Monster's initial, robotic witness description into something decidedly, well, monstrous. Most classic depictions showcase a high midcentury creature straight from a double feature. The evolution of the story also includes the added detail of the death of Lemon's dog, which, according to key witnesses Ed and Fred May, didn't actually occur.

The oddest thing about Flatwoods, in my opinion, is how absolutely natural it should be. If we, as a planet, are expecting true extraterrestrial visitors, we should be expecting robots, drones, or biological entities completely covered by intense protective equipment. Flatwoods would seem to be a perfect example of this; however, the problem is that the Flatwoods Monster is far more of an outlier than the norm in UFO-occupant encounters.

Science dictates that true extraterrestrials should look nothing like us, whereas ufological lore is populated by humanoid beings that, though odd, usually correspond to our basic physiology. This is one of many nails in the coffin of the extraterrestrial hypothesis, and nothing is more damning than that lack of protective gear or breathing apparatus observed on these little humanoids. Instead of spacesuits, many accounts detail beings dressed in little caps, in tunics, or in the nude. This would seem to point to the concept that UFO occupants may not be extraterrestrial biological entities at all, but something else entirely.

The amazing thing is that the initial account showcases a behavior by most witnesses: that of attempted rationalization. When the posse first happened upon the entity, their initial thought – even in light of the fact that they were chasing down some strange thing in the sky – wasn't "giant robot from outer space". Instead, it was "raccoon or possum".

Flatwoods is also a great example of the tendency for local legends to collect other accounts. Another case reviewed in this book, Case 8: The Marlinton Encounter, involved a decidedly Sasquatch-like creature and included other similar sightings in the area at the time. However, given its proximity to Flatwoods, it was simply lopped into the Braxton County Monster of great fame, regardless of actual description. Loren Coleman has noted this snowball-like effect of local legends in his book *Mysterious America*, specifically regarding the infamous Jersey Devil. In spite of the fact that the initial tales describe a ridiculous, winged kangaroo-like monstrosity, later accounts of Bigfoot and pretty much anything else in the Pine Barrens were included under the umbrella of the Devil's bat-like wings.

In the case of Flatwoods, the creature now affectionately referred to as "Braxxie" certainly casts a long shadow.

CASE 3

THE LOVELAND FROGMEN

Yes, you read that right. Frogmen, plural. As if one frogman wasn't enough for the small town of Loveland, Ohio...

The infamous Frogman came hopping through Loveland on the icy night of March 3, 1972. Police officer Ray Shockey was driving around one o'clock in the morning when he saw what he believed was an injured dog alongside the road. As he slowed the car just in case poor Fido decided to jump ahead of him, he suddenly realized that the thing he was observing wasn't exactly what he first thought it was.

Instead of an injured dog, the thing turned out to be a four-foot-tall, bipedal, lizard-like creature covered in leathery skin. The thing looked at him, turned, and jumped over a guardrail onto the river embankment below.

Shockey called his dispatcher and continued on to the police station. Later on, along with another officer, they checked the area with flashlights and found that something had indeed scraped the side of the hill that led into the river.

Two weeks later, Shockey's partner, Mark Matthews, had a very similar encounter. He thought, exactly as Shockey did, that he saw an injured animal by the roadside near the river, so he stopped his vehicle. The thing ended up being identical to the creature reported by Shockey. It stood up on two legs and stepped over the guardrail, eyes fixed on the officer in some amphibian versus human staring contest. It then turned and ran into the river. Matthews claimed that he actually took a shot at the thing – and this is where the story takes a turn.

At the time of the events, Matthews claimed that he must have missed it, and that the frogman lived to croak another day. However, after a couple of decades of sworn silence on the part of the officers, the story changed. In later interviews, Matthews claimed that he did indeed land a shot on the creature, which turned out to be a sickly iguana. However, Ray Shockey himself would later refute that in an interview for James Renner's book *It Came from Ohio...True Tales of the Weird, Wild, and Unexplained*, standing by his initial claims that the thing was truly anomalous.

———————

HOWEVER, fantastic as these decidedly classic cryptozoological sightings are, the story doesn't start there.

Rather, it started seventeen years previous in the spring of 1955. As confirmed by a later news report detailing a different sighting, this event occurred in the early morning hours of May 25. A short-order chef by the name of Robert Hunnicutt was driving home from work around 3:30 in the morning when he saw a truly bizarre sight a mere five minutes outside the town of Loveland on the Madeira-Loveland Pike.

As quoted in Bloecher and Davis's *Close Encounter at Kelly and Others of 1955*, Hunnicutt thought he was viewing "Three crazy guys praying by the side of the road." Much like Shockey and Matthews would do seventeen years later, Hunnicutt slowed his vehicle and realized that he wasn't dealing with three crazy people – he wasn't dealing with people at all.

Instead, Hunnicutt was face-to-face with three beings that he could sum up in two words – "Fairly ugly."

He claimed that the little entities stood about three and a half feet tall and were lopsided, with the right side of their chest markedly larger than the left, and the right arm longer than the left. Their skin was a grayish color, and Hunnicutt believed that they wore a garment the same color of their skin that was tightfitting on the torso and baggy on their legs. Their faces may be the root of the frog-related moniker – Hunnicutt claimed that they had a large, straight mouth that cut across the entire bottom part of their face and lacked any lip musculature. They had no visible nose or eyebrows, but eyes described by Hunnicutt as normal. To top it all off, in place of hair, they had corrugated lines on their foreheads like when baby dolls have that plastic hair texture.

Of the three creatures, one was standing in the front, closer to the shoulder of the road. This foremost figure had its arms above its head, and in its hands held an object described by Hunnicutt as like a rod or chain, which emitted blue-white sparks. He claimed that the sparks actually jumped from one hand to the other. Hunnicutt actually left his vehicle to get a better look at the creatures, at which point the first figure lowered its arm and let go of what it was holding near its feet. It looked to Hunnicutt as though it tied it around its ankles. Simultaneously, all three figures turned to face him.

Somehow not dissuaded or unnerved, Hunnicutt took a few steps towards the beings. The distance between the creatures and his vehicle was about ten feet, and as he began moving around the front of his car, the creatures made another simultaneous and deliberate motion towards him. Hunnicutt actually described it as "graceful".

He then received the impression that he shouldn't come any closer. Hunnicutt also claimed that he had previously gotten the impression that they were focusing their attention on some spot in the woods across the road. He would later state that he believed he had intruded upon an "operation" in which the first figure was somehow using the spark-emitting object to signal something in the woods.

Throughout the duration of this encounter, Hunnicutt was not afraid of these beings, simply amazed. He claimed that, when he finally left, it was simply to go get another person to witness these extraordinary creatures. However, as he started on his way, it would soon be a different story.

Upon getting in the vehicle, Hunnicutt became aware of the strong odor of fresh-cut alfalfa with a slight trace of almonds, an odor that he and his girlfriend would also experience several months later. As he drove away from the area, the terror of his experience began to hit him – according to some accounts, there was even a possible lapse in consciousness – so, around four o'clock in the morning, he stood on the doorstep of Loveland police chief John Fritz to report his encounter. Chief Fritz would vouch for the man's honesty – for one thing, he was satisfied that Hunnicutt had not been drinking, and for another, he claimed that Hunnicutt "looked as if he'd seen a ghost."

"Looked as if he'd seen a frogman" just doesn't have the same ring to it, I guess.

Interestingly enough, on the same night, the Loveland Ground Observer Corps had a sighting of four anomalous objects in the sky.

Hunnicutt's wouldn't be the last strange humanoid encounter of the year. In either late June or early July, nineteen-year-old Carlos Flannigan, a volunteer policeman for the Loveland Civil Defense, was driving back into town. As he crossed a bridge over the Miami River, he noticed four small figures, about three feet tall and moving oddly on the riverbank, as well as a terrible odor. Immediately, he drove to the station to report the incident.

The response to this encounter was interesting to say the least. The police claimed to have no involvement, but the chief coordinator for the civil defense and head of the Loveland Ground Observer Corps, Frank Whitecotton, said that the police had indeed put a cordon up around the bridge when they heard of the encounter. Oddly enough, there were even rumors of FBI involvement.

Around the same time as the bridge sighting, there was another encounter in the upscale neighborhood of Loveland Heights. One Emily Magnone and her husband were awakened in the middle of the night by their barking dog. The couple got up and checked the house. Although they saw nothing, they definitely smelled something – a terrible, swamp-like odor that was reportedly so bad that the Magnones decided to close their windows despite the warm weather. However, it was to no avail – the smell continued, as did the barking of their dog.

While the Magnones had no visual sighting of anything strange, their neighbors certainly did. The next morning, a neighbor lady told Mrs. Magnone that she and her husband had also been awakened by the dog and went to check if anything was the matter.

The neighbor lady went to her back porch and looked out. About fifteen feet away was a little man, about three feet tall, covered in twigs or foliage – this calls to mind the later description of Wetzel's Riverside Weirdo as being covered in leaflike scales. But as strange as that aspect of the creature was, it was hardly the oddest thing about the little man; when the woman turned on the porch light, the creature vanished. As soon as she turned it off, it was back. She tested the reaction out a few times, each with the exact same results. We can only wonder if she left the light on or off when she finally retired to bed.

The Loveland gnomen, as they were referred to in Vallee's *Passport to Magonia*, exhibit some of the strangest characteristics observed throughout entity encounters. The first thing to stand out is the asymmetry of their forms, with one side markedly larger than the other. Several of the reports throughout this book refer to a marked abnormality of proportion observed on anomalous entities, and this is no exception. Thinking outside of the nuts-and-bolts box, it seems in these accounts as though the image of these creatures has been translated improperly, causing the being to appear disproportionate or warped.

The luminous chain held by the front entity finds its parallel across other accounts, including the mirror of the Cussac Devils and the attire of Trasco's Space Leprechaun. The inclusion of shiny or luminous objects either held by the entity, as part of the entity, or somewhere on the entity's outfit or person comes up time and time again in encounters of each different field of paranormal study.

Hunnicutt's reported calmness at viewing these creepy little creatures is not unheard of. From cases as varied as Manwolf sightings to alien abduction accounts, experiencers report an external, almost forced atmosphere of peace – in spite of the fact that they are viewing something that they, quite often, later find to be terrifying or repulsive. Hunnicutt was no exception – it seems that, as soon as he left the area of his encounter, the true abnormality of his experience came crashing down around him.

The scattering of reports observed in this case is a great example of what can be expected in UFO or creature flaps. Often, instead of a single object or entity type being observed by multiple people, there are vastly different things being spotted. In this case, Loveland played host to three strange accounts of entities throughout 1955; however, it wasn't three sightings of asymmetrical gnomen. Instead, it was one account of asymmetrical gnomen, one account of short, nondescript humanoids by a bridge, and one account of a "foliage-covered" being that appeared and vanished at the flick of a switch. Instead of one entity responsible for multiple sightings, we have two wildly distinct sightings and one nondescript one. In addition to that, too, we have the inclusion of a sighting of UFOs.

The sighting at Loveland Heights also involves the interplay of light – and I'm talking mundane, human-sourced light here – with paranormal phenomena. Keel notably was able to contact meandering nocturnal lights using a flashlight in the events of *The Mothman Prophecies*, and light is used to varying degrees as a deterrent in spectral and occult manifestations.

While it may be tempting to say that the neighbor lady's sighting of the disappearing creature was purely subjective, even hallucinatory, as with many cases of entity encounters, it can't simply be written off. She reacted to the objective occurrence of the Magnones' dog acting up, just as the Magnone couple was awakened. Too, there was also the swampy scent detected by the Magnones.

Scent plays an important role in all three of the 1955 encounters, with Hunnicutt's repeat experience of the almond-alfalfa smell, the noxious odor encountered by Carlos Flannigan, and, again, the rank, swampy scent in the Magnone case. As odd and varied as the appearance of each different humanoid was, they certainly shared one common denominator – whatever they were, they smelled.

A FINAL NOTE regarding the later, infamous sightings of '72 – while it is my personal conviction that a sickly iguana is an unlikely candidate for the bipedal, frog-like creature described, even if said iguana was responsible for those encounters, the 1955 encounters are something else entirely. That being said, just what is it about Loveland that made it prone to two short-lived waves of little humanoids?

CASE 4

THE KELLY LITTLE SILVER MEN, OR THE HOPKINSVILLE HOBGOBLINS?

The case of the Kelly-Hopkinsville encounter is one of the most oft-referenced accounts of UFO-related entities, a true classic of anomalies literature. The amazing thing is how the entities themselves sit at a border between two different vernaculars of belief – the decidedly ufological Kelly Green Men (though, as we'll see in a moment, the creatures were actually silver), and the absolutely folkloric Hopkinsville Goblins.

A man by the name of Billy Ray Taylor and his wife, June, were staying with the Sutton/Lankford family at their farmhouse near Kelly, Kentucky in the summer of 1955. On August 21, he went outside to retrieve water from a well when he claimed to see a silver spaceship shooting out rainbow-colored flames. The object moved through the sky, then stopped suddenly and dropped into a gully behind the farm.

When Billy Ray returned to the house and informed

everyone of what he'd seen, they thought he was joking. The entire household, at that time, consisted of eleven people: eight adults and three children. Not one among them went to investigate.

It was mere hours later that everyone in the home, with the exception of June Taylor, who was too frightened to look, would observe the now-infamous little silver men. However, the main stars of this case are undoubtably twenty-one-year-old Billy Ray; twenty-five-year-old Elmer "Lucky" Sutton; his brother, twenty-one-year-old J. C. Sutton; and their mother, fifty-year-old Mrs. Glennie Lankford.

Around eight o'clock that evening, the family dog began acting up and promptly dove under the house, where it remained until the following day. Lucky looked outside and noticed a strange glow in the fields, which appeared to move towards the house. Lucky was soon joined by Billy Ray, and together they saw that the light was caused by a little man floating through the air towards the home.

The beings that harassed the Sutton household on that night have become icons of midcentury UFO sightings. They were described as being about three and a half feet tall, with bulbous, bald heads, pointed ears, huge, unblinking yellow eyes, slit mouths, and spindly limbs. This first being had its arms held over its head, and the arms terminated in clawlike hands. The skin appeared silver and, when in shadow, seemed to be self-luminous. The entity was gliding in the direction of the back door.

Lucky and Billy Ray promptly grabbed their weapons – for Billy Ray, a .22 rifle, while Lucky used the "old duck gun", a 12-gauge shotgun – and blasted at the strange little creature. However, instead of appearing wounded, the creature flipped over onto the ground and ran off into the shadows.

As the two men turned to go back inside, another entity identical to the first appeared at a side window. J.C. promptly shot through the screen and, again, the creature flipped over, this time floating gently into the shadows.

The three men went to check and see if they had actually gotten either of the creatures, and as soon as they stepped outside, the remaining members of the household saw a clawlike hand reach off the roof and grab Billy Ray's hair. Alene Sutton pulled him inside as Lucky opened fire. The creature tumbled off the roof, floated gently to the ground, and ran off – just as another entity appeared in a tree near the house, and yet another came from around the corner.

Strangely enough, the witnesses claimed that the creatures, which appeared as a dull metallic color when in the light, would respond to loud noises, such as being shouted or shot at. The body would increase in luminosity.

Regarding the metallic look of the entities, Mrs. Lankford would remark in Bloecher and Davis's *Close Encounter at Kelly and Others of 1955*, that "It looked like a five-gallon gasoline can with a head on top and small legs. It was a shimmering bright metal like my refrigerator."

Their method of running once on the ground was odd

– the witnesses claimed that they dropped to all fours, and that their arms propelled them more than their legs, which appeared jointless and inflexible. Too, their locomotion was described as incredibly fast.

However, the oddest method of movement has got to be their ability to float. One notable example recounts how the family heard a scraping on the kitchen roof. Upon investigation, one of the entities was moving up on the housetop – the men shot at it, and it floated all the way to a fence post about forty feet away. The men took another shot at it, at which point it fell off the fence and scrambled off into the weeds.

There were several points throughout the evening when the Sutton brothers and Taylor believed that they had succeeded in driving the strange creatures off – only to have the bizarre beings float up to the house once more. The family claimed that they dealt with six separate waves of these creatures when they decided to pack everyone up and go to the Hopkinsville Police around eleven o'clock.

The police were immediately convinced of the serious-ness of the encounter based on the sheer terror of all the witnesses, including Billy Ray Taylor, whose heartbeat had increased to 140 bpm. Soon enough, the Hopkinsville police, state police, and newspeople flooded the Sutton household. However, the only thing out of the ordinary was a patch of luminous grass, which vanished upon closer inspection. Chief Greenwell and all the investigators deserted by 2:30, leaving only the residents. They decided that, as there seemed to be no more disturbances, they would finally retire to bed for the night.

As soon as the lights were out, however, the creatures returned. According to Isabel Davis's investigations, catalogued in her and Ted Bloecher's book, *Close Encounter at Kelly and Others of 1955*, Mrs. Lankford had been attempting to sleep around 3:30 on her bed in the living room when an entity approached the window. When asked how close it was, Mrs. Lankford replied, "Close enough to put his little clawy hands on it."

The household would be harassed by more of the little glowing men in much the same fashion as it had been, and the men would continue firing at the little beings with the same success rate as before. Finally, a half hour before sunrise, the creatures left for good.

Later, a report would come in from a neighbor to the Sutton household, who told a friend of the family that, early that infamous Sunday evening, he'd seen lights moving in the fields behind the farmhouse. This sighting was purportedly between 7:30 and 8:00, just around the time the first of the beings showed up at the farmhouse. An additional neighbor would confirm hearing the gunshots to investigators, giving an objective confirmation that *something* was going down at the Sutton/Lankford farm.

Skeptics of the incident – which included an "unofficial" investigation by none other than members of Project Blue Book – were fans of two theories. The first was that the witnesses were drunk. The initial investigators at the scene, Chief Greenwall among them, searched to no avail for evidence of excessive drinking. What they found, instead, were frightened witnesses in a household that, under Mrs. Lankford's rule, did not allow liquor.

The second theory was the classic scapegoat – the circus. Sometime before the incident, it was postulated, a train full of monkeys had gone rogue and infiltrated the Sutton/Lankford farm. As to how these monkeys were able to float, be impervious to gunfire, or glow silver remains unexplained – not to mention that there was no traveling circus in the area at that time.

There is one final fact before we get on to theory. As pointed out by John Keel in *The Eighth Tower: On Ultra-terrestrials and the Superspectrum*, the nearby town of Hopkinsville does have an odd claim to fame as the birthplace of famed clairvoyant Edgar Cayce, "the Sleeping Prophet".

As mentioned before, the Kelly-Hopkinsville encounter is a mainstay of ufological lore. The strange thing about this is how much of an outlier it is regarding typical UFO-related entity behavior. Considering the similarity of the Kelly entities to the infamous Grays of abduction lore, it's odd that, if their intention was to get in the home, they didn't merely show up in the home. Spindle-limbed, big-headed entities are a mainstay bedroom invader, so in this case it's intriguing to see them acting in such a physical manner. The invasion of the home in waves calls to mind a similar invasion by similarly bullet-proof Bigfoot from Stan Gordon's book *Silent Invasion*.

However, maybe invasion wasn't their intent. Mrs.

Lankford is reported as believing that the little beings were "attempting to communicate" – by the end of the night, she even begged her sons to quit shooting at the little creatures as, she is quoted as saying in Bloecher and Davis's *Close Encounter at Kelly and Others of 1955*, "The things weren't doing us any harm."

The impish look of the Kelly entities led to one of their monikers – the Hopkinsville Hobgoblins. The glowing aspect of their skin is noted in later entity encounters; luminosity seems to be a major part of paranormal phenomena, no matter which field of research you gravitate towards, and will be discussed throughout this book.

One of the strangest aspects of this encounter is this – where exactly did the little beings go when the police and reporters showed up to investigate? True, there was the strange luminous patch of grass – as well as curious, dubious reports of a "whistling" meteor in the area – but the main attraction, the entities themselves, was nowhere to be found.

Researchers such as John Keel and Patrick Harpur have suggested that paranormal events often seem to be staged solely for the witness – could this explain why, in certain circumstances, once the key witnesses have involved others, outsiders, so to speak, the event itself vanishes? Abrupt arrivals and departures are evident across many encounters, including some throughout this book like the Cussac Encounter with Devils and the Weird Winterfold Wonder.

CASE 5

JOHN TRASCO MEETS THE SPACE LEPRECHAUN

On the evening of November 6, 1957, a paper mill worker by the name of John Trasco returned to his home in Everittstown, New Jersey, and promptly went outside to feed his dog, King. According to all accounts, King was a large, nasty-tempered dog who, at the time of the succeeding encounter, was tied up by the side of the house, barking furiously.

While Mr. Trasco went about delivering King's meal, his wife happened to look outside the kitchen window and saw what she first took to be a puddle of water reflecting the sunset, positioned in front of a barn about sixty feet away from the house. She soon realized that she was, instead, looking at a luminous, egg-shaped object, between nine and twelve feet long, hovering a few feet off the ground. Unfortunately, her view of the underside of the object was blocked by some foliage.

What Mrs. Trasco couldn't see was a strange little

man, about two and a half or three feet high, with a putty-colored face and large, frog-like eyes. He wore a green suit with shiny buttons, gloves with shiny objects at the tip of each finger and, most notable, a green hat in the style of a tam-o'-shanter.

Mr. Trasco was face-to-face with a strange entity that, in his words, looked "like a leprechaun".

But the little man didn't just stand there – he had business to attend to. Trasco claimed that his voice was "sharp and scary", with language he referred to as "broken" and "as if he came from the other side". Whether this refers to England or the afterlife is up for debate.

The space leprechaun said, "We are a peaceful people. We don't want no trouble. We just want your dog."

Although Mrs. Trasco couldn't see the action, she certainly heard her husband's reply. He yelled, "Get the hell out of here!"

Surprisingly enough, that's exactly what the little green man did. He marched right into the object, though no entry point was visible. The object in turn took off straight into the sky in a manner described by Mr. Trasco as "like a flame".

When Mr. Trasco came back inside, he apparently had green powder on his wrist. One account includes the claim by Mrs. Trasco that her husband had attempted to grab "one of them", a detail that implies, though this is nowhere explicitly confirmed, that there may have been more than one entity involved. This powder supposedly came off when washed; however, more of the powder appeared under his fingernails the next day.

The next night, two stationary lights appeared over the residence before vanishing completely. Mrs. Trasco, concerned at this reoccurring incident, is quoted as saying that she wishes her husband would have let the little green man have the dog, as it was "so cross she couldn't think of anybody else who would want it".

While this case alone is strange enough, it is, as of yet, incomplete. The same day that John Trasco of Everittstown, New Jersey, was facing down a frog-eyed space leprechaun intent on taking his dog, in Dante, Tennessee, a young man by the name of Everett Clark claimed that four entities also attempted to catch his dog, Frisky. In this case, however, the four entities – two men and two women – appeared like normal human beings speaking a language similar to German. When they, like the space leprechaun, failed to apprehend Frisky, they filed into their own luminous, oblong object through no visible entry point.

Intriguing how two separate encounters occurred on the same exact date, both involving the botched abduction of a dog, and in both cases the entities entered a luminous craft through no visible entry point. The wordplay between the place name of Everittstown and the witness's name of Everett is just one of those vexing synchronicities so prevalent in unexplained research. However, the strangest aspect of these two cases is the fact that, for all these similarities, the entities observed were absolutely different.

Clark's encounter dealt with normal-looking, German-speaking astronauts, terrestrial as far as he could tell. Trasco's encounter was a little green man with glowing buttons on the tip of each finger. Does this mean that the space leprechauns and the secret German-speaking spacemen are dog catchers for some great dog pound in the sky? Or simply that the image is less important than whatever lies behind it, that the same show must go on regardless of the players?

To quote one of John Keel's widely published newspaper articles, "Cattle Rustling in the 20th Century – Strange Things are Happening to Animals", "There is a growing suspicion among ufologists that pied pipers from outer space are also zeroing in on dogs."

It's a commonly held belief across the paranormal, as well as folkloric traditions, that dogs can see or sense supernatural entities. From the natural concept that a dog would be aware of a large animal like Bigfoot, to the age-old notion that dogs can see ghosts, we also see this crop up in the Fairy Faith, where countless accounts detail dogs going up against the Good Folk, usually to protect their master or master's property. Of course, with both the symbolic and genuine role of dogs as guardian, it seems to be no surprise that "the other" would see fit to remove this barrier however possible.

Given the apparent success of the entities throughout the alien abduction narrative, I find it odd that in both these cases the beings failed at their objective – implied in the Clark encounter, stated in Trasco – which was absconding with the dog. I find it even more odd in light of the unhappy fates of many domestic animals that happen to be around unexplained occurrences – again, dogs seem to be an especial target.

However, both King and Frisky lived to bark another day.

Trasco's space leprechaun also exhibited a strangely common detail on its clothing – shiny objects, here observed as buttons on the shirt and the fingertips of the gloves. The importance, and prevalence, of luminous phenomena in entity encounters will be discussed at length in a later chapter, so hold on to your tam-o'-shanters.

Trasco's defense warrants discussion here as well. Although his wife claims that he tried to "grab one of them", an intoxicatingly vague nod to the possibility that there may have been more than one entity, the little green man was dissuaded from his quest simply by Trasco yelling at him to "get the hell out". This direction of intention correlates to both attempts at resisting alien abduction, as well as some methods of dealing with haunting-type activity. Of course, the success of these methods varies from experiencer to experiencer. This sort of defense also comes up in one of the greatest catalogues of the Good Folk.

From Evans-Wentz's *The Fairy-Faith in Celtic Countries* comes an account in which two men looked across the river and saw small beings in a circle of light. The reporting witness wanted to move closer, but his friend suggested they continue on their way. The friend struck a roadside wall and shouted, at which point the circle of light and the beings vanished instantly. The parallel between the shouting of that witness and Trasco are evident, as is the parallel between the fairies' circle of light and the space leprechaun's luminous object.

Another aspect ties this UFO occupant to the spectral – the green powder. While, first and foremost, this is a fantastic example of a physical artifact left behind after a bizarre and dreamlike experience, the fact that it was a powdery substance ties it to many accounts of "powder" or "ash" being left at the scene of spectral manifestations. One of the most dramatic was an account from Keel's *The Complete Guide to Mysterious Beings*, in which a woman had a classic bedroom invasion, waking to see a monk-like figure standing over her bed. While this could be written off as a hypnagogic hallucination, it's a bit more difficult to explain what happened next. She reached out to touch the figure's outstretched arm, and it crumbled into powdery ash.

In conjunction with the decidedly leprechaun-like look of Trasco's entity, this powdery substance calls to mind a decidedly folkloric substance: fairy dust. While fairy dust may seem like the stuff of fairy tales and not the Fairy Faith, ties between the Good Folk and dust, powder, or ash do go back to age-old traditions involving one of the fairies' preferred modes of transport – whirlwinds or dust devils. Additionally, according to John Rhys's *Celtic Folklore: Welsh and Manx*, there are several cases of the Good

Folk vanishing in a shower of dust. Different methods of protecting against enchantments have to do with the throwing of dust, as well as multiple accounts of the fairies throwing dust in the eyes of those they wish to hide from. In conjunction with the getup of Trasco's little man, I can think of no other case that so clearly ties our modern little green men to the green little men of antiquity.

CASE 6

1958 was a banner year for Bigfoot. Heck, 1958 was when the term "Bigfoot" was coined by the *Humboldt Times*, and Sasquatch fever ran rampant during that time frame. Which may be why Charles Wetzel's encounter with a scaley, beaked biped has consistently been tossed in the Bigfoot bin.

On the evening of November 8, 1958, Charles Wetzel of Bloomington, California, was driving near Riverside, where North Main Street crosses the normally dry Santa Ana riverbed. On this particular night the river had overflowed, and at a dip in the road, water was actually running across the pavement. As Wetzel crossed this aquatic area, his radio began transmitting static. Changing the channels produced no effect, but that would soon be the least of his concerns.

Wetzel saw what he first took to be a sign by the roadway before realizing that he was, instead, face-to-face with a six-foot-tall, bipedal creature with a "round, scare-crowish head like something out of Halloween", which, though lacking both ears and nose, had a protuberant, beak-like mouth and fluorescent eyes. The entirety of the creature was covered in scales, which Wetzel told reporters were "not like a fish, but like leaves".

Wetzel also claimed that the creature seemed "off" – yes, it's some enigmatic, scaley biped lurking on the road-side, there's not much room for normality there. However, witnesses to creatures from Hellhounds to ghosts often remark on proportional abnormalities, an added anomaly to already anomalous beings, and this case also exhibits this trend. Wetzel claimed that the legs appeared stiff and were not set under the beast's torso, but came out from its sides. It also appeared to be waving its long, spindly arms. One report quotes Wetzel as saying the arms were "longer than anything he'd ever seen". Throughout the whole duration of the encounter, Wetzel claimed that the creature was making a bizarre noise halfway between a high-pitched scream and a gurgle.

To make matters even worse, this creature proceeded to run into the road, where it stopped right in front of Wetzel's vehicle. It reached across the hood and clawed at the windshield. As it did so, Wetzel grabbed his pistol but decided not to shoot the creature. If you thought this was out of the kindness of his heart, you'd be mistaken.

Instead, he rammed on the gas and ran the beast over as its screeching intensified. It tumbled forward and then went under the car. Wetzel claimed that he could actually hear his vehicle scrape over the creature, and later investigation revealed that not only did the underside of the car exhibit marks that it *had* recently run something over, but the windshield also had long, sweeping claw marks.

The papers referred to the creature as "Wetzel's Wisp", aside from the *San Bernardino County Sun*, which cleverly coined it "the Abominable Noman". According to the local police department, the matter of the Abominable Noman was quickly put to rest by the discovery of a pair of fake costume feet about a mile away. However, if Wetzel's sighting was of some hoaxer in phony feet, it raises the question; where did they end up?

Wetzel claimed he could actually hear his car scraping over the monster, and the physical evidence corroborated that point – after all, s*omething* had scraped away the grease on the undercarriage of his vehicle. If that something was a hoaxer, that would simply mean that he had run over some guy in a Halloween costume point-blank. Given these circumstances, it seems unlikely that said hoaxer wouldn't turn up, likely in a hospital.

There was another sighting of a dark humanoid figure by another motorist in the same area the next day. In this case, police bloodhounds searched the area to no avail.

The two events that immediately preceded Wetzel's sighting are of interest – the fact that he crossed over water, and immediately his radio began transmitting static. The effect on the radio, while there's no way to prove it was caused by the creature, there's also no way to prove that it wasn't, and the importance placed by Wetzel on this disturbance certainly makes it seem that he believed it was connected. However, the crossing of the waterway is an angle I find of great interest.

The connection between paranormal beings and water or waterways is a double-edged sword. Many researchers have commented on water as serving as some type of "battery" for paranormal entities and occurrences, and waterways certainly run rampant in monster, UFO, and haunting-heavy locales. On the other end of the belief spectrum, there are multiple traditions involving the inability of supernatural entities to cross running water.

Symbolically speaking, I think that whether viewing water as a deterrent or boon to supernatural beings, the importance of it is in what it represents. According to Jung in *Collected Works of C.G. Jung, Volume 9, Part 1: Archetypes and the Collective Unconscious*, "Water is the commonest symbol for the unconscious." Too, across countless world mythologies, waterways, namely rivers, form the boundary between worlds, including but not limited to the well-known River Styx, the River Gjoll of Norse mythology, the Huber of Mesopotamian, or the Apanohuaia of the Aztecs.

Looking at such accounts of paranormal entities seen near waterways or, in the case of Wetzel, seeing a paranormal entity *immediately* after crossing running water, is this indicative of the witness "crossing over" from this world to some other?

On the flipside, is the traditional belief ascribed to certain entities as being unable to cross over waterways a giveaway that their appearances may be sourced purely in the collective unconscious, whereas others freely traverse this bound? Admittedly, this is pure speculation, but given the possibility that paranormal entities have some connection to the human mind, it is speculation worth entertaining.

Also, the Wetzel encounter also brings up the notion that the appearance of anomalous entities may be tied to symbolic figures or archetypes. The description of the creature as having leaflike scales calls to mind the motif of the Green Man, a leaf-adorned being that appears as a symbol across multiple cultures. This sort of symbolic and archetypal reference shows up across paranormal encounters and may be evidence that the event is tied to human consciousness, particularly the collective unconscious.

CASE 7

FLIX, THE CREATURE THAT MADE A NAME FOR ITSELF

There are cases that have everything, and then there are cases that have everything *plus* claims of a Scooby-Doo-style ploy. Flix, or the Ghost of Conser Lake, falls into the latter category.

Conser Lake is something of a ghost itself now – it's currently on private property somewhere in Linn County, Oregon, near the towns of Millersburg and Albany.

The first occurrence in this area to mark the beginning of this strange saga was a sighting by a mint truck driver sometime in 1959. He claimed that a creature that resembled a shaggy, white gorilla kept pace with his truck, traveling about thirty-five miles per hour, even looking inside the cab. It only vamoosed when he neared the mint distillery.

Other accounts from this time detail sightings of a massive, bulletproof "something" that screamed like a cat and left massive footprints in the area. One newspaper article detailing the beast also refers to a "flying saucer" that supposedly crashed into Conser Lake that year. On September 10, the *Corvallis Gazette-Times* discussed a UFO sighting from the nearby town of Albany in their column "Off the Beat", claiming that over half a dozen people had spotted an erratic light maneuvering through the sky.

THE CASE that brought the Creature of Conser Lake to the forefront came, as so many cryptid encounters do, from a group of teenagers. Seven of them, to be exact, six guys and one girl. On the night of July 31, 1960, the group was near the shores of Conser Lake when two of the boys got the bright idea to sneak around and jump out at the rest of their friends. As they began to execute this plan, they heard a loud crashing noise and soon enough saw what was making it: a seven-foot-tall, white-furred creature, described by some of the group to look like a polar bear and others a white gorilla. Perhaps strangest of all was its eerie cry, described by the witnesses as a high-pitched "Fleep! Fleeoweep!" One of the boys included the strange detail that it made a squishy noise as it walked, something like wet shoes.

One member of the group, George Hess, reported the creature to the sheriff, while the other kids returned to their homes only to return to Conser Lake with a posse of gun-toting monster hunters. Over the course of the next couple of weeks, Conser Lake was not just haunted by the monster – which would gain the moniker "the Ghost of Conser Lake" due to its pale hue – but also by countless people looking to shoot the creature, whether with a camera or a gun.

The creature wasn't the only one in danger here. One teenaged boy who was simply out fishing on Conser Lake had one hell of a close call when he heard one of the very last things you'd want to hear in a monster hotspot – "There he is!" In short order, two bullets narrowly missed his noggin. Local papers carried article after article begging people to please, PLEASE be careful when hunting the monster.

However, the creature wasn't restricted solely to the banks of Conser Lake. Reports came in from all over the area, whether sightings of the creature or trace evidence such as large, webbed, duck-like tracks. Local farmer Clarence Starr claimed that the monster had trampled down the better portion of his mint harvest, and he wasn't the only farmer in the area to have experiences with something unknown. An editor's note in the August 19 edition of the *Greater Oregon* says, "The Creature of Conser Lake has been seen by too many farmers and visitors in the area to deny that he exists."

MRS. PENNING, a resident of Dever Conner, north of Albany, claimed that she found strange fingerprints on her bedroom window following an odd series of events that began with the noise of dripping, like a leaking rainspout, one fine, dry August day. Gradually, the dripping noise turned into a low-pitched cry that gained pitch before tapering off. Upon looking out the window, she saw a large, light-colored figure with furry paws.

Two weeks after this odd sighting, Mrs. Penning and her sister were home for the evening when they heard rapping noises coming from first one window, then the other. At this point, they discovered odd, wide prints of a palm and perfectly parallel fingers on the window.

The creature certainly was busy throughout the summer and early fall of 1960. Sometime in mid-October, one of the first teens to spot the creature, Marilyn Samard, had an additional sighting in the company of her mother, aunt, and two boys. The group had just left the home of Mrs. Penning when they decided to stop near Conser Lake. Suddenly, something appeared from behind a nearby garbage dump – I'll add that garbage dumps are one of a series of locales pinned down by John Keel as areas with heightened creature and UFO activity. The witnesses started up the car and began driving away, only to have the creature, claimed by Marilyn to be identical to the creature she saw way back in August, appear again. Only this time, it began circling the vehicle, even peering inside, though, strangely enough, no facial features were visible.

Around this time, there was also the mysterious killing and shredding of two hound dogs that had been set after the mysterious beast.

However, the most interesting angle of this entire affair is the persistent belief of multiple local residents that the Conser Lake Monster had telepathic abilities. Witnesses claimed headaches after their meeting with the creature, or a peculiar silence settling over the area prior to their encounter. As we'll see in a moment, there are claims of far more sensational telepathic communiques.

BETTY WESTBY WAS responsible for many of the articles throughout the Conser Lake Monster scare, often describing in detail her treks out into the area surrounding the lake, looking for the creature, and usually finding instead groups of kids with shotguns.

However, one account of her adventures truly stands out.

She decided to bring along, as she put it, "a local telepath", who informed her that the creature "doesn't like to be called a monster".

When pressed for a better title, the entity (through the telepath) replied that "visitor" or "alien" would suffice. Westby wondered if he'd object to creature, and he replied that he wouldn't.

So from then on, the Creature of Conser Lake it was.

BUT AMONG THE lengthy telepathic conversation had between the psychic and the creature, in which he discussed how he meant no harm, came only with affection for the creatures of Earth, and was lonely, the creature came up with an even better name. When asked specifically what he was called, the entity replied, "I am called Flix. There are many like me, but I am the one called Flix."

Surprisingly enough, this wasn't the only claim of Flix-sourced telepathic messages around. One Alvin Hammock claimed that he, too, had received a psychic message from Flix. He set out to look for the creature, but first projected out that the creature didn't need to fear him. Shortly, he was rebuffed with the snarky (telepathic) reply, "How do I know I can?"

Hammock assumed that this was a reference to the jackknife he was holding and, in an effort to make Flix more comfortable, decided to ditch it in the car before heading out into the wilderness.

On his way back to the car, Hammock claimed that he had to grasp a limb to step over some water and was shoved – by no one. By this point totally spooked, Hammock ran the rest of the way to his vehicle. About halfway there, he glanced back to see if he was being followed and saw some grass flatten into a perfect, twenty-inch-diameter circle.

While reports of the creature continued, it wasn't long before Flix became old news.

HOWEVER, some years later, there is a report of the true Holy Grail of all cryptid encounters, the sort of thing that can only make you shake your head and say, "Zoinks." In the *Albany Democrat-Herald* from October of 1964, under the article entitled "Falsity Clings to Life", comes this: around the time of the Conser Lake Monster scare, authorities in the area discovered an illegal cache of liquor on the shores of the lake. Naturally, it was assumed that the sightings of the monster were due to some Old Man Jenkins type dressing up to scare away those meddling kids.

Needless to say, if that is in fact the case, that plan sorely backfired. Not only did initial sightings ignite interest in the creature, but teenagers invaded the Conser Lake area – and not just a few meddling kids and their dog. At one point, it's claimed that over two hundred people were parading through the area at one time, cameras and shotguns in hand.

Much like the silver-painted monkeys of Kelly-Hopkinsville fame, this explanation leaves a lot to be desired. Front and center are the earlier sightings from around the greater Conser Lake area, such as the 1959 encounter of the mint truck driver. His sighting of a shaggy white gorilla correlates to further sightings – but he was nowhere near the banks of Conser Lake and that illicit liquor stash.

Also, considering that many sightings occurred after the area was literally littered with trigger-happy teenagers, it makes the costume idea a bit more than slightly foolhardy – it would be downright dangerous.

One of the most intriguing cases from the height of the creature scare was the series of two sightings had by Mrs. Penning. The rapping, first at one window, then at the other, is indicative of poltergeist phenomena. The leaving of prints also has its spot in the lore of poltergeists and hauntings.

The account reported by Marilyn Samard and friends directly after leaving Mrs. Penning's home includes the odd detail of facelessness. This has been observed in multiple sightings of hairy hominids – Momo, the infamous Missouri Monster of Louisiana, Missouri, is likely the most recognizable – as well as across other paranormal manifestations.

The flattening of the mint fields, as well as the claim of actually witnessing a twenty-inch circle of grass depress under some unseen force, ties closely to our modern concept of crop circles and traditional beliefs regarding mowing devils or fairy rings. It's intriguing, too, to see how this case was treated across many different belief systems – the papers entertained talk of psychics, UFOs, someone even claimed that Flix floated like a ghost.

However, the showstopper in this case is undoubtably the telepathic communication. Regardless of the inherent factuality of such statements, the fact that at least two people claimed to receive telepathic messages from this being, in addition to further claims of more vague psychic effects such as headache, is intriguing and not the first claim of this sort in relation to a hairy hominid. An albeit very different type of telepathic exchange can be found in

Stan Gordon's *Silent Invasion*, in which a witness claimed possession by an inhuman entity, and throughout the works of Linda Godfrey, usually involving close encounters of the creepy canid sort.

What stands out about Flix's rapport is that it followed a pattern nearly identical to UFO channeling, even with Flix's preferred moniker of "alien" or "visitor". However, the sci-fi double-feature connotations don't stop there, with such statements of "affection for the creatures of Earth" and "I mean no harm" sounding more in line with a little green man in a tin can than a giant, white-furred gorilla-like creature with webbed feet and a propensity to harass mint farms.

CASE 8

THE MARLINTON ENCOUNTER

It's not uncommon for experiencers of odd phenomena to wait on reporting their sighting, if they opt to report it at all. Their reasons for doing so usually have to do with fear of public humiliation and ridicule – W. C. Priestley, better known by his nickname "Doc" Priestley, had concerns that were not so pedestrian. Doc Priestley waited until January 1961 to report his October 1960 sighting of a very odd Sasquatch-like creature, but not for fear of what the public might think.

No, Doc Priestley stated that he didn't want to scare his friends away from going deer hunting with him later in the season.

The friends in question, Gene Williams Forest and Mont Priestley, had been leading the way in a camping bus with Doc following behind in his vehicle. They were traveling through the heart of the Monongahela National Forest to do some turkey hunting in the Williams River area of West Virginia. Near the small town of Edray, about three miles north of Marlinton, Doc Priestley's car, which, according to multiple accounts, had been "purring like a kitten", began to sputter. It came to a complete stop.

Priestley looked to the roadside to his left and saw a "monster" with long hair standing on end. Priestley sat there for a time, paralyzed by fright, until finally his two companions noticed that he was no longer following them. At the approach of the camping bus, the monster "dropped his hair" and ran off. Priestley's car started again, and the trio continued on their way. He decided not to tell his friends about the sighting.

However, it was not long before Priestley's vehicle again began to sputter, only this time, sparks were visible flying from under the hood, and it appeared the vehicle was having a bad short. The car stopped, and there, by the roadside, was the monster, hair raised as before.

How long Priestley sat there a second time is unknown. Eventually, his friends noticed he was, yet again, falling behind, and backed up the bus. Again, the monster disappeared. However, the vehicle didn't start back up – the points had been completely burned out.

Newspaper accounts quote Priestley as saying that the reason he didn't "tell the boys about this was I wanted to go back up there deer hunting and knew they would not go with me if they knew about what I had seen."

ALTHOUGH PRIESTLEY'S is one of the most engaging accounts from this time, it is by no means the only sighting of the strange creature. On December 30 of 1960, a twenty-five-year-old bakery truck driver by the name Charles Stover claimed that he saw "the thing" around eleven o'clock in the evening. As he rounded a curve on a backwoods road between Braxton and Webster counties, Stover claimed that he saw a six-foot-tall hair-covered creature standing bipedally in the road, "glaring" at his vehicle. He almost hit the beast, stopped to get a look, and then fled the area. Stover was so upset by the incident that he sped down the road and didn't stop until he found a filling station restaurant, where he ordered a cup of coffee to calm his shaken nerves.

At the restaurant, one thing led to another, and soon enough a posse, complete with shotguns and rifles, organized and returned to the area to look for the monster. Although they didn't find the monster, they did find upturned rocks and marks in the ground.

Weird cries and other sightings continued to plague the area for some time, and the intriguing thing is that all of these sightings of a decidedly Bigfoot-like creature were instead lopped into the Braxton County Monster of great fame. Perhaps better known as the Flatwoods Monster, we visited with this high-midcentury monstrosity in Case 2 of this book. Completely different in both context and appearance, it just goes to show how easily occurrences become legends become catchalls. As *The Raleigh Register* of January 5, 1961, put it, "The Braxton County 'monster' is back again and apparently is branching out."

This mild monster panic continued around the area to varying degrees for about a half year – there's one account from August of '61 of a seventeen-year-old boy becoming so scared of "something" that he ran full-tilt down a road, finally smashing through the window of a barber shop. Needless to say, by that point in time, the local police departments were less than enthused about creepy creature sightings.

While the sightings in this time frame were of a classic hairy hominid nature, the car stoppage experienced by Doc Priestley is truly unexpected, though not unprecedented. Sasquatch-like creatures have been tied to electromagnetic disturbances, even vehicle stoppages, such as a very similar case from Yakima, Washington, in September of 1966, in which a man's car stalled after seeing a silver-furred Sasquatch in the road. Although not a hairy hominid, the decidedly lizard-like weirdo of Wetzel's encounter has a tenuous tie to radio interference – whether this was exclusively due to the creature is not certain, though it certainly is coincidental.

Of course, vehicular frying is probably more closely linked to close encounters of the ufological kind, and electromagnetic effects and electronic failure have been tied consistently to haunted locations.

In this case, the response was simply so immediate. The vehicle starts having issues – the creature is spotted. The creature's hair "drops", and the vehicle starts up again;

the first time around, at least. The second time, Doc wasn't so lucky.

The detail of the hair standing on end is of interest and pops up in other, more conventional sightings of Bigfoot. Researchers often point to this detail as similar to the piloerection, or bristling of hair, associated with anxiety and aggression in many different mammals. In this case, however, it seems as though the raised position of the hair was timed intrinsically with the effects on the vehicle.

This brings up an interesting concept. The hair seemed to be affected by the presumed electromagnetic field disturbance. While this doesn't answer the question of whether the creature caused the disturbance or was also affected by some outside disturbance, it shows that the creature was not exempt from the effects of the electric charge. However, the camping bus was not subject to it – it seemed to exist solely between Doc Priestley's vehicle and the hair-raising monster.

Regarding Priestley's encounter as well, yet again the creature was only observed by him. However, the effects of the encounter are as objective as they come; his car was fried.

CASE 9

SIMONTON'S FAMOUS FLYING FLAPJACKS

As if three self-proclaimed "UFO Capitals of the World" weren't enough, Wisconsin also lays claim to one of the most offbeat, highly strange, simply random encounters of ufology, the Simonton Encounter.

...or, as J. Allen Hynek remembered it in *The Edge of*

Reality: A progress report on Unidentified Flying Objects, "the man in Wisconsin with the pancakes".

Joe Simonton wore many hats; he was a plumber, chicken farmer, and, around Christmas time, local Santa Claus for the small town of Eagle River in northern Wisconsin. At around 11:00 in the morning on April 18, 1961, he was eating breakfast when he heard a strange noise coming from outside. He described the noise as "like knobby tires on wet pavement" and went outside to find the source of this bizarre disturbance.

Hovering some feet above his backyard was a bright silver object, about twelve feet tall and thirty feet in diameter. He claimed that its shape was like two inverted bowls with exhaust pipes six or seven inches in diameter spaced around its edge. One really couldn't ask for a more classic, midcentury flying saucer.

A hatch opened in the side of the object, and Simonton saw three men inside. He later told investigators that they looked clean-shaven, "Italian-looking", and short, each one standing about five feet tall and wearing black turtlenecks with black, knit helmets.

The interior of the object was described as being dark, compared by Simonton to the color of wrought iron, which contrasted sharply with the "brighter than chrome" exterior. One of the entities stood nearest the hatch, its outfit differentiated by a white track stripe running down the side of its pantleg. It gave Simonton a little jug, which he said looked like a "thermos" and seemed to be comprised of the same color as the exterior of the craft. Simonton took that to mean that the being wanted water.

In light of the fact that there was a literal flying saucer hovering over his lawn, piloted by three turtlenecked pilots, Simonton decided not to be unneighborly towards these otherworldly guys – he went into the house, filled the jug with water, and returned it to the being.

He continued studying the interior of the craft and noticed several instrument panels and the sound of a generator-like hum. He also saw one of the beings cooking something using a type of flameless grill. Simonton motioned his interest, and the track-striped entity responded by handing him three of the infamous "alien pancakes". Though referred to as pancakes or cookies throughout articles, these small discs bear only the slightest resemblance to the breakfast food. Photos of the pancakes, including Simonton holding one, show small, three-to-four-inch discs liberally perforated with holes.

The entity then attached some sort of belt to a hook in his clothing, which retracted him back into the object. The hatch closed, leaving no impression in the object's exterior, and then the whole kit and caboodle took off in a southern direction. Simonton claimed that there was actually a disturbance that bowed some of the nearby pines.

Simonton immediately contacted the sheriff, a man he had known for fourteen years. Again, Simonton was a well-respected member of his community, and multiple people, including Vilas County judge Frank Carter and local newspaper editor Dan Satran, vouched for Simonton's character. Judge Carter brought up a valid point across multiple papers; in addition to Simonton's respectability, he just couldn't see any motivation or benefit to making the whole thing up. As a matter of fact, Simonton would lament across later articles that he had lost three weeks of work to this affair and that, if he saw another flying saucer in the future, he'd keep it to himself.

Following the initial investigation by local authorities, the Air Force stepped in to do their own investigation, including sending one of the infamous flapjacks off to the Food and Drug Laboratory of the US Department of Health Education and Welfare. The pancakes were found to include not Martian flour or moon dust, but simple, terrestrial ingredients. According to the Air Force's findings, catalogued in Vallee's *Passport to Magonia*, these included "hydrogenated fat, starch, buckwheat hulls, soya bean hulls, and wheat bran".

Which is lucky enough for Simonton, who, barring fears of alien viruses or radiation poisoning, had actually *tried* one of the pancakes. His conclusion was that it tasted like cardboard.

This was the final nail in the coffin; Simonton's case was signed off by the Air Force as "psychological", the predominant belief being that he had enacted a waking dream involving spacemen and pancakes, even making the disgusting, cardboard-tasting discs himself.

However, Jacques Vallee took a greater interest in this case than the Air Force did, noting several great similarities between Simonton's case – and his cake – and multiple accounts from the Fairy Faith of the British Isles. Surprisingly enough, in Vallee's eyes, it was that very piece of evidence – the pancake – so damning to the saucer hunters, that strung Simonton's report along the wider tapestry of folklore.

For some reason, cakes and baked goods – specifically flat breads or, yes, pancakes – have a long history throughout otherworldly encounters. The Fairy Faith stands chief among them, with such cases referenced by Vallee including details that the cakes were made, as Simonton's were, with buckwheat hulls. Vallee also mentioned the curious detail that Simonton's pancakes were devoid of salt and that, per many traditions, the fairies would not eat salt.

However, fairies are not the only sort of otherworldly contact believed to involve pancakes. Vallee also cited a case of purported demonic infestation from Father Sinistrari's *De delictis et poenis*, which was begun with a mysterious pancake. On the opposite side of the pearly gates, the symbolic importance of flat or unleavened bread is rife throughout the Judeo-Christian belief systems.

Another aspect of Simonton's encounter in line with folklore and mythology worldwide is the request for help or assistance, in this case the request for water. This is a common motif throughout myth, legend, and religion; it also has its odd place among anomalous entity encounters. A chilling example of this can be found in Linda Godfrey's book *The Michigan Dogman,* in which a woman reported her friend falling into a trancelike state upon witnessing a hellhound-like creature along a roadside, even slowing the vehicle. Later, the friend remarked that the creature was "in her head", saying that "it needed help."

Speaking of the request for water, Simonton's spacemen carried with them a container that appeared to be comprised of the same material as their craft. This stylistic tie between entity and craft is something mentioned by Paul Devereux in his book *Earth Lights* as possible evidence that the so-called UFO occupants and UFO are comprised of the same substance. More on that later.

Although the pancakes are undoubtably the wackiest aspect of the Simonton Encounter, the appearance of the entities themselves also captures a balance between the mundane and the whimsical as to warrant a closer look. The turtleneck and track-stripe combo calls to mind the fads of early sixties fashion, while the knit caps or helmets strike up the old folkloric chord of the pointed caps associated, even today, with fairies, imps, and goblins. This balance between mundane modernity and whimsical folklore of ages past captures the paradoxical nature of anomalous occurrences, which at once seem to contain objective patterns regardless of culture while also exhibiting a reflective ability to mimic a person's personal or cultural belief systems.

CASE 10

THE THREE-RING CIRCUS OF CISCO GROVE

September 4 of 1964, a twenty-six-year-old family man by the name of Donald Shrum had accompanied two of his friends and coworkers to do some bow-hunting at Cisco Grove in Placer County, California. Unfortunately for Mr. Shrum, at one particular ridge the trio became separated, and as it was nearing dark, he still hadn't joined up with his two companions, Tim and Vincent. It was later uncovered that Tim was the only one who managed to find their camp; he waited a while, then set off to find his friends, only able to locate Vincent. Strangely enough, Vincent claimed that he had seen an odd, slow-moving "meteor" streak through the sky. However, this would be far, far from the weirdest sighting of the evening.

The two men returned to camp and figured, wisely enough, that it was then too dark and too late to go searching for Shrum. Being a capable outdoorsman, he should have been fine fending for himself for the night.

Meanwhile, Shrum came to a very similar conclusion. After realizing that he was most definitely lost, he wisely decided not to try wandering around in the dark underbrush. Reports of bears in the area foremost in his mind, he found a large tree growing near a granite outcropping, climbed up into the branches, and resigned himself to an uncomfortable night's stay.

Shortly after perching in the tree, Shrum saw a white light below the horizon, moving in an east-to-west path but maneuvering up and down as it traveled. Shrum at first believed that it was a flashlight or lantern, until he saw it go over a tree. Then he figured one of his friends must have contacted the forest service, and this light was a helicopter coming to his rescue.

He jumped out of the tree and quickly lit three signal fires, then began waving his arms to flag down the rescuers. Suddenly, this "helicopter" turned and headed straight towards him. It was at this moment that Shrum realized that this was some helicopter – for one thing, it was absolutely silent.

Upon realizing that the light only appeared to be about eight to ten inches in diameter, Shrum came to the somber conclusion that the only other thing it could be was a flying saucer. Given the size of the light, however, he also came to the conclusion that it must have been "just a little dinky thing". Little dinky thing or not, Shrum decided that it would be wise to head for the safety of his tree and stay perfectly still. The object moved past him and finally hovered over a nearby canyon, giving Shrum a clear view of the entire object.

He later estimated the ship to be about 150 feet long. Although its edges were indistinct, he said that the stars were blotted out in a roughly oval-type shape. The most noticeable part of the object was a series of three flat, illuminated rectangular panels arranged in formation.

He would later refer to this object as the mothership, and about five minutes after it resumed this position, something was expelled from the center panel with a flash. Shrum claimed that it was a "dome-like affair", complete with a blinking light. Its trajectory was such that Shrum believed it landed about half a mile away from him, and soon enough, he heard something crashing through the underbrush towards his direction.

Shrum didn't have to wait long to see what was making this noise. A short time later, a bizarre figure approached the area. He claimed that it stood a little over five feet tall and wore a tight, one-piece, silver uniform with odd "puffs" at the joints. Shrum claims that he couldn't tell if it was wearing headgear or not, though its face seemed flat and very dark. Although Shrum mentioned that it seemed to have a nose very low on its face, the most evocative feature was its large, dark eyes, which Shrum compared to welding goggles. These eyes would later be the topic of nightmares for the frightened witness.

As soon as the creature was in view, it began messing around with a manzanita shrub nearby. It came within a hundred feet of Shrum's tree when it was joined by another creature identical to itself. This caused him to panic – Shrum claims that his mind turned to how the heck he was going to survive this situation, and he tried to remain as still as possible up in the tree. He contented himself with the notion that the foliage, combined with his camouflage outfit, should keep him safe from view. However, that sense of security would immediately be dashed to bits as one of the entities moved to the base of the tree. The second entity followed, and they both stared up at him with their large, dark eyes.

Thus began an ordeal that lasted the entire night. Interesting to note here is that, throughout the whole encounter, Shrum claimed that he heard cooing and hooting noises, which the entities reacted to. When they heard this noise, they would turn to face the mothership, and maintained that the whole night it seemed like they were receiving some sort of communication. However, Shrum stated that he wasn't sure if the noise was specifically related to the entities, or simply an owl. Regardless, for the rest of his life, Shrum would become highly anxious at the sound of owls hooting, directly relating it to his traumatic experience.

As if two entities weren't bad enough, suddenly a third entity emerged from the brush. The first thing Shrum noticed was its huge, bright eyes. Shrum claimed that this being looked robotic, complete with a metallic uniform with jointed fingers and a square, hinged jaw mechanism. Its face was illuminated by fiery, red-orange eyes. Shrum would consistently refer to this being as "the robot", and the others as "the humanoids".

As the robot approached the two humanoids, it brushed away the dying embers from the middle signal fire. This was the beginning of Shrum's troubles.

The robot reached up to its mouth and released a cloud of white vapor, which, though odorless, had an immediate effect on Shrum. He began gasping and blacked out; when he came to, he still felt nauseous and even dry-heaved. Bow in hand, Shrum did the first thing that came to his mind and decided to fire at these beings. He later stated that he felt he could have killed either of the two "biological" entities and didn't want to do that, so he decided to fire instead at the metallic robot. He shot an arrow at the chest of the creature, and when it made contact, there was a bright flash of light. The robot was driven back about two feet. The entities all scattered, but soon enough the trio returned to the base of the tree. Shrum was able to fire twice more, to the same lackluster effect, before running out of arrows.

Recalling how the robot had swept away the dying embers, Shrum lit a book of matches and tossed it down on the ground. This had an immediate and surprising effect; not only did the three entities back far away from the little fire, but Shrum claimed that even the ship shot straight up in the sky. Taking note of this effect, Shrum then proceeded to light everything he could on fire, tossing each object down as the previous one burned out. Through the course of the night, he ripped up and burned through his camouflage clothing, his hunting license, all the money he had on his person, and even his hat. Each time the fire waned, the entities would creep back, retreating as he threw down the next article.

By the end of the night, he was left wearing only his jeans, T-shirt, shoes, and belt.

Truly out of options, Shrum climbed further up into the tree and lashed himself to the trunk with his belt just in case he was gassed again.

That was a good call – soon enough, the same odorless vapor attacked him, and he passed out. When he woke up, he saw the two humanoids attempting to climb the tree in a nearly laughable manner. One entity tried to boost the other up into the branches. Shrum attempted to shake them out of the tree, and as soon as they felt this slight movement, the humanoids jumped down. The robot returned, released the odd vapor, and Shrum blacked out. When he came to, the humanoids were back at the base of the tree, trying to climb up...

This charade continued all night, pausing only several times when Shrum threw down his remaining, nonflammable objects; his canteen, which the creatures inspected and tossed away, and the loose change he had in his pockets. The beings expressed a deep interest in the coins, even taking them away at the end of the encounter.

The two humanoids and one robot weren't the only beings involved in this account. Shrum claimed that there were at least three or four other humanoids, identical to the initial two, in the area. These kept busy combing through vegetation, apparently taking no interest in him.

Sometime throughout the night, another robot-like entity joined the scene. Right before dawn, the two robots moved close together, facing each other at the base of the tree. The entire area became illuminated by flashes of light, which arched between the two beings. Suddenly, a huge cloud of vapor approached Shrum, and he, unsurprisingly, passed out.

When he came to, all the entities, the craft, and his loose change had all vanished.

Exhausted, he finally managed to find his way back to camp. Not only did Donald Shrum have physical effects linked to his night up in the tree, such as a major cold and a bruised chest from rocking the tree against him, he also had lasting effects from this occurrence likened to PTSD. His terror throughout the duration of the encounter is evident – he claimed that when the entities were continuously besieging his perch on the tree, his only thoughts were on how to survive the incident, and whether he would live to see his family again. Though he spoke to several people about this experience, he resolutely tried to stay out of the limelight for fear that he would be laughed out of his job.

Two weeks later, he did revisit the site and was able to locate two of his arrows. He claimed that it had a "glob" of something metallic on the end, but that it was then taken by the Air Force.

Speaking of the Air Force, they did indeed investigate this case. Their first suggestion was that Shrum had run into one of those infamous packs of teenaged pranksters – complete with inflatable flying mothership and a can of knockout gas. When Shrum wouldn't agree to said theory, this case was signed off with the same conclusion as the Simonton Encounter: psychological. However, from all reports Donald was considered to be an average, sane person, not the sort given to making up ludicrous tales of flopped alien abductions. On that note, if this was a hoax, props to Mr. Shrum for risking pneumonia by spending the night belted to a tree after burning his cap and coat, not to mention any paper bills on his person. That takes some dedication.

Speaking of burning money, Shrum also refused sums of money for this story, resolutely desiring to keep it out of the press for the longest time. He maintained major concerns about losing his job, which, incidentally, was working as a welder for the Aerojet General Corporation. At the time of his encounter, his company even held contracts with the United States government, helping in the construction of rocket engines.

Shrum's experience is considered a classic case of UFO occupant contact, and he believed that it was the intention of the entities to take him, falling in line with the much-popularized concept of alien abductions. However, the question remains; why did they fail so completely, pathetically even, at taking him? Not only did they possess a knockout gas, which was effective enough to render Shrum unconscious, the massive mothership was, supposedly, hovering right nearby. In light of later beliefs regarding abduction lore, it seems odd that these entities would prove to be so incompetent at capturing one measly human being stranded in the middle of nowhere, right down to the nonsensical attempts to climb the tree.

The fear of fire exhibited by the entities, particularly their retreat when the fire burned brightest and drawing back when it burned low, calls to mind the behavior of Sasquatch from certain accounts involving fire, as well as similar responses from ghosts or perceived occult entities regarding, more specifically, a hatred of light. The single strangest aspect from the Shrum encounter, though, is the combined response of the entities and the craft; when the entities drew back, the craft did as well, when they returned, it returned. Could this be evidence that the appearance of the separate entities plus the mothership was simply that – appearances – enacting out the same function?

Considering that, according to the extraterrestrial hypothesis, the mothership must have traversed massive stretches of space to get here, there's no practical reason that the tiny flames caused by books of matches or even a burning hat – a good fifty yards away from its position, at that – posed any sort of threat to it.

The last method of defense employed by Shrum, the throwing of coins, exhibits one of the strangest aspects of this case. The tossing of small objects in the direction of a supernatural entity immediately calls to mind a very similar defense used against witches, vampires, and, some-times, even the fairies in which people would scatter salt, grains, or other small objects in their direction, claiming that the being would not continue on their path until the objects were counted. In Shrum's case, the entities were absorbed with the coins until, apparently, pocketing them. Though tenuous, I am also reminded of Charon's Obol, the tradition of placing coins with the deceased as payment for their passage into the land of the dead.

Shrum's belief was that they just liked them because they were shiny.

Later investigators would remark on the gathering of coins as evidence of that midcentury trope – aliens researching this planet. This was also mentioned in conjunction with the beings as they "messed around" with a manzanita plant. Where recent generations see extraterrestrials gathering samples, previous generations saw fairies and elementals tending to the natural world. Each concept is a reflection of the current mode of thought, and who's to say which one is truer. The same concept of study was thoroughly believed by Shrum, who believed that the entities were simply here to study the Earth and that, when they saw him, plans changed.

Like so many encounters, this experience was ushered in by a light anomaly. The first thing Shrum noticed was the light, which he thought was a helicopter moving through the trees; this was the catalyst for the entire event. Every major escalation in this encounter was also punctuated by the presence of lights. When the "dome-like affair", believed by Shrum to carry the entities, appeared, there was a flash of light. The first thing noticed about the robot, by far the most troublesome aspect of this case to Shrum, was its bright eyes. And, finally, at the end of his experience was the dramatic display of arching light between the two robots.

While on the topic of lights, it seems important that Shrum lit three signal fires in an attempt to flag down the infamous helicopter-that-wasn't. When the mothership was observed in all its glory, it had three luminous panels. The center signal fire was purportedly put out by the robot; the center panel was the one that disgorged the dome-like object. Oftentimes, when a rapport is first established with paranormal entities, notably ghosts, the call is for repetition – to repeat the same sequence of knocks, for example. In this case, perhaps the repetition of threes is coincidence – or perhaps evidence that the image used was reflecting Shrum's own setup of three lights.

It can't be stated enough that Shrum did experience lasting effects from this affair, notably symptoms relating to PTSD. One of the most pronounced of these effects was his lasting fear at the sound of owls. Owls as a screen memory are a common belief throughout ufology, specifically abduction lore. However, the notion of owls having additional importance has also been noted by researcher and experiencer Mike Clelland. In this case, Shrum was unable to decide whether the hooting or cooing sounds that the entities reacted to were from owls or not; regardless, he maintained that fear throughout the rest of his life.

CASE 11

WALL DONUTS, WATERMELON CLOUDS, AND WALKING STUMPS

Kathy Reeves of Pioneer Mountain, Oregon, was only fifteen when strange things began happening to her and her family in March of 1966. Little did she know on that particular evening, as she and a friend were walking back to her home, that their experience would serve as the catalyst for a long-running series of truly bizarre encounters.

Kathy and her friend were walking on Pioneer Road when they noticed a ruddy glow. Assuming it was a fire in a neighbor's field, they approached the area cautiously and saw that it was, in fact, a burning, dome-shaped object. Kathy described the light within the domed confines as looking "like smoke boiling".

Wisely enough, the duo decided to continue on to Kathy's home. However, they were soon assailed by yet another light, which appeared like a flashlight with a cover on the end so that there was no projecting beam, just a circle of flat light. Kathy had made up her mind that someone was playing a trick on them, so she decided – unwisely enough – to chuck a rock in the direction of the light. As soon as she did so, a series of large lights immediately came on all around the small round light, and the two teens ran to Kathy's home and safety.

However, that safety was only temporary. After this initial occurrence, the Reeves' family home was soon host to near-constant strange phenomenon. Nightly, strange pulsating lights referred to by the witnesses as "wall donuts" visited the residence, accompanied by a high-pitched whining noise. Both of these were observed by Deputy Sheriff Thomas Wayne Price when he was called to the home on numerous times. He described the motion of these donut-shaped lights as "crawling" across both the interior and exterior walls of the home and said that the noises sounded like a high-speed saw or giant, spinning top.

Light anomalies were in anything but short supply at the Reeves residence. On March 30, a friend of the family, chemist Max Taylor, had agreed to camp out on the lawn to see what he could make of the strange lights. In the middle of the night, he called up Sheriff Price to say that there were two pulsating, blue spots of light on the Reeves house – one at one end of the house, the other at the opposite end. The effect was that some beam of light was actually piercing the home; however, no beam or other light source was visible.

By the time Price arrived at the scene at around 1:20 in the morning, half a dozen people had gathered in the yard to watch the strange light anomalies. As soon as Price set foot out of his vehicle, he looked up and saw a large, glowing orange object performing maneuvers in the sky. The same whirring noise started, and the object vanished.

And odd things continued to be observed inside the residence as well. In the early hours of one morning, Mrs. Reeves was awakened to find that her bedroom was filled with a rosy, pinkish light, bright enough that she could have read a newspaper, she claimed. She turned to move into the living room and stopped short. There, hanging in the doorway, was a watermelon-colored cloud, filmy enough that she could see through it. It lasted for several seconds and then vanished.

On another occasion, a family member actually went for their gun after seeing an ambiguous "something" through the living room window. As soon as he took aim at whatever it was, it appeared to retreat. However, it seems that the Reeves traded one anomaly for another – as soon as the thing vanished, the interior of the home was filled with "crawling lights".

The high point of this case, however, is something that many investigators at the time seemed not to care about so much. Those walking tree stumps. I first ran across this case in John Keel's classic work, *The Complete Guide to Mysterious Beings*. And, with a slight date change, I was able to locate the article he mentioned from the *Spokesman-Review*, October 18, 1966, "Oregon Puzzlers: Strange Things Are Happening".

At this time, the activity had been going on a little over

six months, and Kathy Reeves, by then sixteen years old, was quoted as saying that she had witnessed "the three little stumps that walked across the pasture".

They must have changed color, because Kathy stated that they were orange, light blue, white, yellow, and "watermelon-colored" – don't ask me what the Reeves family had with that particular descriptor, because I don't know. Both *Flying Saucer Review* and *The A.P.R.O. Bulletin* reported on the Reeves case, and in both articles singled out the stumps as the least interesting part of this case.

Which is near tragic, as I can think of few other accounts so odd.

The Reeves family ended up packing up and moving because the activity was just too prevalent. The man who purchased the house, one Mr. Delbert Mapes, claimed that the activity ended soon after. However, at least one report details that he had sheets tacked up on the windows for some time to keep out the light from round, luminous objects ranging from an inch to thirty inches in diameter, which still plagued the property.

Of course, he could have been referring to the stumps, which had, apparently, decided to make a like a tree and leaf.

While Kathy stated that her home had never had these sorts of manifestations until the incident with the dome-shaped, seething light and the unfortunate decision to throw a rock in the direction of the beamless flashlight, the Reeves household was not the only spot where odd activity was happening in this area at the time. As a matter of fact, people were seeing strange stuff in the sky, as well as other anomalies, all over the place. One person reported spotting a house-sized glowing sphere. Another came forward to describe their sighting of a revolving string of Christmas tree lights, while another said they saw an oval-shaped object topped with a dome and searchlight. As with most UFO flaps, it's not that there is a single object responsible for all sightings. Rather, in this case, it seems as though there was a steady background of luminous anomalies, plus these more bizarre descriptions of other objects.

Or entities. The cops informed the papers that there was one account they didn't take too seriously. Someone had reported a cyclops.

Now, in light of the hefty UFO presence in the area, the Reeves family disturbances were discussed mainly in terms of UFOs – for the most part. None other than para-psychologist Dr. J. B. Rhine, coiner of the term ESP, came forward to say that the inclusion of lights in this case bore a strong resemblance to many European poltergeist and spirit light cases. At the time of the initial instances, Kathy Reeves was only fifteen, and it's conventionally thought that poltergeist agents tend to be teenaged girls.

The inclusion of the high-powered saw noise is also indicative of poltergeist occurrences, which in modern times often include mechanical noises, while older cases compared such sounds to the noises of a winding clock or the winding of a jack. It also brings to mind the screeching of Point Pleasant's infamous Mothman, which according to one witness screeched like a bad vacuum belt.

Across the works of many investigators, UFO witnesses sometimes develop poltergeist-like manifestations in their homes. If this is the case, the initial sighting of the fiery dome by Kathy and her friend can be looked upon as the kickoff to a series of escalating activity that finally culminated in the Reeves family moving away.

The flap that was occurring in this area included many different types of unidentified aerial phenomena (not to mention that pesky cyclops). However, it does seem that the Reeves household was especially "haunted". Kathy herself would maintain the belief that she had inadvertently started the activity by throwing the rock at the anomalous lights.

Was this interaction the catalyst for the heightened activity at her home, even in the midst of an otherwise active UFO flap? The odd thing is that the throwing of a stone *by* a witness is an inversion of many typical accounts. The throwing of rocks and other small objects has been chalked up to nearly every type of paranormal entity – poltergeists, fairies, and Bigfoot included. However, in this case, it was the witness herself chucking a rock at the unknown that seemed to be the event to usher in a real era of high strangeness.

CASE 12

THE CASE OF THE CUSSAC DEVILS

On August 29, 1967, two children had been tasked with supervising about ten cows grazing in a meadow outside the small village of Cussac, France. Francois Deleuch was thirteen at the time, and his sister Anne-Marie aged nine. They passed the time by playing cards and were accompanied by their little dog, Medor.

Around 10:30 in the morning, the cows up and decided that they wanted to cross a low stone wall into a neighboring field. Francois got up to lead them back when he noticed that, on the other side of the road past a hedge, stood four "children" whom he didn't recognize.

Several newspaper accounts of this case mention that he called out, "Would you like to come play with us!" While adorable, this is unfortunately a journalistic fabrication. Instead, Francois almost immediately realized that these weren't four children at all.

He climbed on top of some stones to get a better look and saw that these four short figures were accompanied by a six-to-seven-foot-diameter, brilliant silver sphere, which shone so brightly that it was painful to look at. By this point, Anne-Marie joined her brother in viewing the strange occurrence across the way. Both siblings claimed that the object had no details on the surface – however, Anne-Marie noticed details like "landing gear" underneath the object. She claimed that she saw three or four straight legs with small round shoes, which immediately vanished when the machine was in flight. This was one of two points in this case where the details observed by both children differed.

In front of the sphere stood the four entities that Francois had first believed to be children. Their heights varied between three and four feet tall, and the tallest entity held an object in its hand that the children claimed looked like a mirror. They were completely black, of a shiny texture that Francois compared to silk, and the children couldn't discern if this was the entity itself or some sort of perfectly fitted, seamless one-piece suit, which also covered the head.

There was no description of eyes, ears, or mouths on any of the entities, though Anne-Marie independently claimed that the tallest entity had a pointed nose. This was the second discrepancy between her report and her brother's. Both children attested to the fact that, although the head seemed to be of normal proportion in relation to the body, the cranium of each being was pointed. In addition to that, they also said that each being had a pointed chin, complete with a pointed beard that was visible on either side of the head and under the chin.

The children claimed that the arms were long and spindly and, although they couldn't make out anything akin to hands, claimed that the feet of the tallest entity were webbed.

The tallest entity waved its hands around as though gesturing to the other beings, one of which appeared to be bending over inspecting the dirt. Eventually, the being furthest to the left of the object went straight up into the air and then dove head-first into the spherical object. The next being did the same, and then finally the third. The fourth, tallest entity rose into the air, dove back to the ground like it was picking something up – Francois believed that it had dropped its mirror – and then finally entered the sphere, which had ascended slightly by this point in time.

The sphere performed a tight spiral maneuver upward, accompanied by a soft yet piercing whistling noise combined with the sound of wind, though the air was still. It continued spiraling higher, growing brighter by the moment, when the area was beset by the odor of sulfur. Both the children's cows and neighboring cows began crowding close together, lowing, and Medor began barking at the strange object. The sound ceased, and the sphere sped off in a northwestern trajectory, but the children didn't wait to see the object move out of sight. They were too busy getting the heck out of there, driving the cows home a half hour earlier than anticipated.

Police were called to the scene and arrived around four o'clock that same day. The smell of sulfur was still present, as was a patch of yellowed grass, which would normalize by the next day. It was later uncovered that a nearby resident, noted in some accounts as an off-duty police officer, had been in his barn shifting hay at the time of the children's encounter and had heard a strange whistling noise.

Those who investigated this case found the children to be sincere witnesses. The parents said that they had come home in tears, Francois unable to sleep that night and Anne-Marie kept up for two nights. Francois also had watery eyes for about fifteen minutes after the incident, and about the same amount of time each morning upon waking for some time thereafter. It was theorized by investigators that Francois was so affected by the sighting due to his eyeglasses, that somehow the luminosity of the object was compounded by the lenses. They also theorized that this is why he didn't notice the "landing gear" or the pointed nose of the fourth entity, whereas his sister did. The smell of sulfur in this case is of some note – in addition to the decidedly impish look of the entities involved, the presence of sulfur in this case directly led to the branding of this case as "Encounter with Devils" in the September/October 1968 issue of *Flying Saucer Review*. However, it's been pointed out by many paranormal researchers, notably John Keel and Joshua Cutchin, that sulfur is heavily associated with every type of paranormal phenomena, not simply relegated to the fire and brimstone of demonic fame.

Discrepancies between eyewitness accounts are always a tricky topic. On the one hand, many researchers regard this as a giveaway that the account is suspect – heck, the witnesses can't even get their story straight. On the other hand, it's reasoned that different individuals pick up on different things. In this case, where both witnesses were children, the overall cohesion of detail is staggering, lending credibility to an incredible claim. The two deviations – of the landing gear and the nose – were thought by investigators to be due to Francois's more delicate eyesight.

However, considering that he was right on the money with all the other details – the beards, the pointed craniums, the webbed feet – this may also be evidence for the concept that events such as these are not solely objective, material events, but rather something that straddles the boundary between objectivity and subjectivity. Another aspect of this case that lends credence to that idea is the claim of the landing gear. Anne-Marie was able to describe it in such detail – but then claimed that it didn't retract into the object upon takeoff, it was simply *gone*. So many paranormal occurrences seem to have faulty transitions, lacking a steady path from point A to point B, and the magical vanishing landing gear is a great example of that.

The performance of the entities is also of note. At the time of this encounter, it was handled by ufologists in a very ufological manner, who did the best they could to figure out the cloaking device used on the craft to make it appear that the entities simply dove into a solid object through no entry point – this behavior has also been observed in the Trasco account and the Clark account from the same day. When confronted with the behavior of the entities messing around with the soil, the claim in Cussac was the same claim used time and time again in so-called UFO occupant encounters – the extraterrestrial was taking soil samples from Earth. However, some centuries before, the sighting of a small, imp-like being messing around with dirt would be accepted as part of the iconography that fairies are connected to the earth, nature, and farming.

Speaking of agriculture, this case also has an icon heavily associated with the Good Folk: cows. Throughout accounts of dealings with the fairies, cows and other livestock are the continual victims of otherworldly charades.

The comparison is easily made between "fairy blight" and "cattle mutilation", as well as the pesky habit of the fairies to relocate livestock.

The object carried by the tallest entity is also of note, and it's curious that Francois defined it as a mirror instead of a bright or reflective object. Objects compared to "magic wands" are observed time and time again in entity encounters – covered earlier in this book is the Hunnicutt encounter of frogman-haunted Loveland, in which a troupe of little gray men included one entity holding onto a sparkling "chain" or "rod". In this case, the pointed cranium and bearded chin call to mind various types of goblin or imp – which, in turn, were literally demonized by Christianity.

CASE 13
THE CONNECTICUT CREATURES

Time and time again, strange entities are defined by the conditions that surround them. A shadowy humanoid in a graveyard is a "ghost", just as the same shadowy humanoid in the woods is a "Bigfoot". Likewise, beings observed in conjunction with any type of aerial anomaly are "UFO occupants", whether they are seen to "occupy" said anomaly or not. Such is the case with the following account.

On September 15, 1967, Carol Luke and Ruth Passini, both fourteen, were hanging out listening to music in Carol's bedroom, located in the second story of her farmhouse on Wallen's Hill Road just outside Winsted. Her mother had gone to the store around 7:30, and the two friends were still awaiting her return when the succeeding event unfolded around 8:45.

Both girls were watching out the window for Mrs. Luke when they saw a brilliant, egg-shaped object the size of a small car about two hundred yards away near a barn complex. They thought at first that it was near the ground, but then realized it was actually hovering in the air. As they watched the object, they claimed that it changed color, running through a spectrum of super-luminous white, to beige, to pink, to deep scarlet, about ten times. The object was absolutely soundless.

However, the silence was not to last long. Suddenly, the girls heard a noise they compared to that of a "power mower when it fires but fails to start" coming from the area of the barn. Immediately after they heard this noise, the two girls saw two small figures come out of the barn and run to a mailbox on the road. They claimed that they couldn't really get a good look at the figures, as by then it was dark out, and clouds kept obscuring the moon. However, they estimated that the figures stood about four feet tall and had abnormally large heads. Carol later stated that she believed, though couldn't absolutely be sure, that one of the figures was more defined than the other and had an even larger head than its compatriot.

The two creatures stayed by the mailbox for a couple of minutes, then ran across the road and hid under a large tree. Headlights appeared, at which point the duo ran back across the road and were joined by another figure identical to themselves. The due-cum-trio ran past the barn and hid while the car passed by.

The girls tried in vain to see the little beings after they vanished behind the barn, but they did see the light once more as it became dimmer and dimmer. They believed that it had begun losing luminosity when the car went by, and by the time Mrs. Luke returned home, it was dim to the point of obscurity.

The two teenagers weren't the sole witnesses to this weird event. Mrs. Pinozza, who owned the lot across the street where the two creatures had run to, affirmed that she too had seen the egg-shaped object, which frightened her so badly that she went into her house, shuttered the windows, and locked the door behind her. Two other adults by the names of M. Morehead and B. Marecki also came forward to say that they had observed the same bright object within an hour of the initial sighting.

Like many of my favorite landing cases, the defining feature of this incident seems to be the nonsensical behavior of the entities involved – which, first and foremost, it's tempting to refer to these little guys as UFO occupants. However, the Winsted creatures bring up an important point – so very many entities are identified as UFO occupants regardless of if they are seen to "occupy" a UFO or not. Many accounts of entities are tossed into the UFO bin even in the absence of any sort of UFO presence in the area at the time of the sighting.

In this case, yes, there was a close sighting of some unexplained aerial phenomena, and there did seem to be a connection between the beings and the egg-shaped object – namely, they showed up at the same time, and the object dimmed when the beings came out of the barn. However, although the entities showed up in conjunction with the object, the only thing they truly "occupied" was the barn!

As in other cases, the entities in this account were ushered in by both a light anomaly and a strange noise, in this case the mechanical sound of a misfiring power mower. Anomalous mechanical noises have their ties to other paranormal encounters, such as poltergeist and other cryptid encounters.

But anyway, back to the nonsense. It's truly intriguing to me that these little humanoids were literally spending their time running around, back and forth across the road. The connection it brings up for me, only highlighted by the rural setting and agricultural ties, is to the lighthearted play of the Good Folk, and to me this is kind of a classic example of that – just with a flying saucer in tow. It also almost seems like a modern play at a very old concept – there are countless stories of the fairies showing up when people are playing music. Here, instead of some peasant with a fiddle, we have two teenaged girls listening to a radio – however, that core concept remains the same.

Another interesting point is that inconclusive comment made by Carol that it seemed as though one of the entities was clearer than the other. Again, for the record she said she couldn't be sure, and it seems that lighting conditions were far from ideal, but the notion remains that there was some variance in the clarity of the entities. Needless to say, I wish that we could have a "clearer" understanding of what she meant by that, as ghosts, fairies, and creatures of all ages seem to sometimes have their image lost in translation.

At its core, this is yet another case of strange entities

accompanied by some light anomaly and, much like the case of the Cisco Grove encounter, it seems as though the entities and the object bear a behavioral connection – responding to mundane lights. In Cisco Grove, both the posse of strange entities and the so-called mothership fled from fire, while in this case, the object dimmed and the entities hid as the car's headlights moved past.

Of course, there are other cases, such as the fantastic selection of personal experiences detailed by John Keel in *The Mothman Prophecies*, in which strange lights, objects, or entities seem to engage with our flashlights, headlights, etc. Safe to assume, though, it seems as though one of the greatest ways to affect a change or response from the phenomena is through the use of lights – which is interesting, considering that, in reverse, it seems as though one of the great icons of high-contact, high-strangeness encounters revolves around the prevalence of light.

The corroborating reports from three separate adults are also intriguing, as it shows that, unless the whole neighborhood was up for a good old-fashioned hoax, something odd did in fact occur. Also, it's really interesting to see the different responses from people – Mrs. Pinozza was so frightened by the egg-shaped object that she ran into the house and shuttered the windows, and therefore didn't see the humanoids, while the girls remained straining at the window even after the entities had vamoosed and the object had all but faded from view.

Symbolically, too, and this applies to so many cases I'd be hard-pressed to compile a list of them, I have major interest in the shape of so many objects as egg-like. This one, much like in the Trasco encounter, doesn't really appear to be a "craft" per se. In this case, of course, the entities never appeared to enter or exit the object, while in the Trasco encounter the space leprechaun simply entered the object through no visible entry point. Mythologically speaking, the egg is often associated with a primordial chaos out of which our plane of existence and order is born, the concepts of life and resurrection – also there's an element of that which is hidden. I can think of no other symbol more fitting for the UFO, one of our age's great puzzles.

CASE 14

THE WEIRD WINTERFOLD WONDER

A little after midnight November 13, 1967, a twenty-two-year-old by the name of Philip Freeman and his twenty-year-old friend, Angela Carter, were driving from Cranleigh to Shere in the district of Surrey. The road they were on was desolate; it passed through wooded, hilly country. It had rained earlier in the evening, the sky retaining a dense cloud cover, and as they had encountered no other cars on that stretch of road, the night seemed very dark indeed.

As the car hadn't been running long enough for the heater to come on, the windows began misting over. So around two miles away from Cranleigh, Freeman stopped the vehicle to clean the windshield.

As he exited the car, he suddenly smelled a strange odor, compared to burnt food or a stink bomb. It was strong enough that Carter also smelled it from inside the vehicle. Freeman finished cleaning the windshield, climbed into the driver's seat, and was horrified to see a "face" through the passenger window, right past Carter. Maybe "face" isn't the right word. He claimed that it was an oblong shape, about ten inches long and eight inches wide, and absolutely blank. This "face" was bright white, and considering that the only lights around were on his vehicle, he believed that it may have been slightly self-luminous.

Freakiest of all, it was lurking just outside the car window. The thing seemed to stand even with the top of the vehicle, about four and a half feet tall. At this point in time, Freeman could only see that the rest of the body was dark, aside from a white "arm" of sorts, which was placed on the car's hood.

Freeman claimed he immediately felt very cold and terrified, which must have translated. Carter had been talking about the disgusting smell as Freeman reentered the vehicle but, when she saw the look of horror on his face, refused to turn around to see what he was looking at, merely telling him to start the vehicle and get out of there.

In the one, maybe two seconds it took Freeman to start the vehicle, the creature moved to the back of the car, its face pressed up against the back window. As the couple sped away, Freeman took a quick glance at the being through the back window and was impressed with the notion that the entity was bell-shaped and lacked any sort of legs.

As soon as they left the area, the smell immediately vanished. They believed the whole encounter only took around two minutes, and no time discrepancies were reported.

Of course, as pointed out both in the *Flying Saucer Review* article by Bowen as well as Joshua Cutchin's fantastic book *The Brimstone Deceit*, the terrible odor associated with this sighting is a common enough occurrence across paranormal fields; interestingly enough, in the article Bowen also connects it to concurrent sightings of mystery cats in the area in the early sixties, which were apparently attended by a strong smell of ammonia.

The arm resting on the hood calls to mind the Wetzel Encounter covered in Case 6, in which the creature scratched the hood of Wetzel's vehicle. Of course, Wetzel's encounter also included radio interference – no electronic effects were reported in this case.

In fact, this case seems to be an inversion of your typical car stoppage. As in the case of Doc Priestley's infamous encounter and commonly exhibited in UFO cases, the vehicle fails, comes to a stop, the creature or object is seen. In this case, there was no vehicular failure or other electronic interference, for one thing, and for another, the witness stopped the car to clean the windshield of his own accord. After the car had stopped, the smell was noticed, and then the creature was seen. Talk about perfect timing – was this thing out for a midnight glide and just happened to come upon Phillip cleaning his windshield? Again, we have that tricky word coincidence – would the same encounter have happened several yards down the road?

I guess the question is – if Bigfoot screams but no one is around to hear it, does it still make a sound? Do these entities still lurk outside the confines of our observation, or are they bound by the observer?

Interesting to note too is the immediacy of everything – there was the burnt odor, which apparently became stronger in the vehicle once the door was opened than it was outside – and, upon getting back in the car, the creature was at the window. Since Freeman believed it was self-luminous, he certainly would have noticed it coming up to the car from the dark roadside. This lack of observation implies that it was simply there. Then, once he was in the vehicle, it was at the back window in a matter of a second – no moving from point A to point B, just here one moment, there the next. And finally, there was no lingering odor once they left the area – it cleared immediately. It seems as though when the couple left the event, everything ceased.

The immediacy of this encounter seems to lend itself to the concept that this event was tied exclusively to the witnesses, mainly Freeman, observing it – unless, of course, some faceless bell-shaped thing with one arm likes to hang around that area waiting for unsuspecting people to wipe their windshields.

One of my favorite aspects of this case, however, is the name coined by Charles Bowen, "the Spectre of Winter-fold". True, it showed up without a saucer, but the strange, ambiguous, nearly mechanical-looking shape still seems rife with UFO iconography. It reminds me of the infamous case of the "tin ghost" observed in the French flap of 1954.

The facelessness of the entity is also an intriguing

concept. Speaking broadly, entities described as faceless or having obscured faces crop up in every apparently different field of paranormal research. One of the most infamous faceless cryptids is Momo, who was described as having hair so long it covered its face completely. A half-step away in description from the Missouri Monster is New Jersey's Morristown Monster, described as a bipedal, seven-foot tall scaley thing with long black hair, which also lacked a face. UFO-related entities often have their faces obscured; there is an excellent case from Zimbabwe in 1981 where a group of several people saw a ball of orange light followed by three or four tall people in shiny metallic coveralls whose faces were too bright to be seen.

The banshee of Celtic folklore was often observed wearing a long veil, and a popular Yokai of Japanese folk-tale, the Nopperabo, is exclusively recognized by its lack of facial features. Classic ghost stories detail faceless ghosts, such as the Gray Man of Pelican Inn on Pawleys Island, South Carolina, or the Faceless Man of Boulthom Park in Lincolnshire. In odd congruency to the banshee there is the ghost of Becontree Station in London, a woman in white with blonde hair and no face. The positioning of this ghost at a station, congruent to the banshee's roadside, the white attire, and the lack of a face makes this seem almost like a modernized version. One of the most infamous types of faceless specter are the ghostly members of clergy – faceless nuns and monks abound, including the faceless nun of Foley Hall in Indiana, and the faceless monk of the Mission San Juan Capistrano in California.

So what does this all mean? Conventionally speaking, not much. The lack of facial features in each separate case are ascribed to separate causes: Momo's face was covered in long hair, the banshee wears a veil, the extraterrestrial was wearing a hood or helmet. However, I think it may point to a different explanation entirely – that these entities may be only partly formed. I'll return to this concept more fully in the conclusion.

Regarding the Weirdo of Winterfold, when we think of this being as this bell-shaped, faceless entity, it reminds me of the silhouette of other famous faceless specters of the more conventional variety, such as the banshee, the woman in white, faceless monks or nuns, just lacking in detail.

Interestingly enough, according to paranormaldatabase.com, a mere fifteen minutes away near Chilworth there is a claim of a faceless cyclist from 1960. However, back to the task at hand, I feel the strangest thing about this concept is this: why would something without eyes press its face against a window as though "looking" in? Regardless of actual form, these things seem to continually perform function after function that may or may not fit them.

CASE 15
THE SHARPSVILLE SHAMBLER

So many cases of bizarre hairy hominids contain earlier encounters of a far more ambiguous sort. This escalation of events from the vague to the definite calls to mind cases of hauntings, which typically start with small disturbances such as weird feelings or strange noises before the appearance of full-bodied apparitions or disembodied voices. The tale of the Sharpsville Shambler exhibits this same sort of pattern.

The story starts in June 1970, with a farmer and ex-marine by the name of Dale King. He had been visiting his future wife at her home in Sharpsville, Indiana, that particular evening when the couple began feeling both physically and emotionally odd. The physical response included intense dizziness and light-headedness, while emotionally, they were each swept with a wave of fear. Finally, they decided they'd try a different atmosphere to escape this bizarre and sudden onset of abnormality and set off for

Dale's home in the country. However, their night soon took a turn from the unusual to the downright strange.

It was already dark out, and the night patched with fog, but ahead of them on the road was an unusually dark area. They actually stopped the vehicle, debating back and forth whether they should turn around or go through this patch of absolute darkness. Finally, they decided to continue on their way, hesitant to return to the strange area of fear that they had been seeking to escape.

As they entered the dark patch of road, the young couple claimed that not only was visibility limited, but their headlights also couldn't illuminate the road ahead of them. Also, within this dark spot, it was significantly warmer than the surrounding area. Finally, as they approached Dale's house, the darkness lessened.

Unfortunately for the couple, they were greeted by yet another surprise. Dale's faithful dog, Zipper, tried to attack them not once, but twice.

As strange as the events of that June night were, all of this was merely a precursor to another series of even stranger events about a year later, in June or July of 1971. One evening, all the family dogs began acting up around 10:00. Zipper, ever the faithful companion, once again takes center stage.

Dale went to see what the ruckus was, and saw that Zipper was busy attacking some bipedal, hair-covered creature, which stood in a low spot in the yard, about twenty-five feet away from the house. Dale stood in the doorway and studied the bizarre creature, which, he claimed, stood about nine feet tall with an oddly shaped head he described as neither ape-like nor manlike, but rather like a large, furry helmet. The being had long arms and was totally covered in dirty, stringy hair.

Dale claimed that it stood in a stooped position and emitted a deep growl as it swung at the dog. The particular actions of this entity are of some note – Dale claimed that it looked like it was moving in slow motion and that it appeared confused or unsure of what it was doing. Zipper would lunge at the creature, which would slowly swing its arm and miss. Then Zipper would hit the ground and jump back again.

Suddenly, as Dale took in this strange sight, the being turned and looked at him.

The only thing more horrifying than the eerie gaze of the creature was its disgusting odor, which Dale compared to decaying meat and vegetable matter. Dale wasted no time in running inside to grab his handy-dandy shotgun, only to realize that it was out of shells. By the time he located his stash and ran back outside, the helmet-headed ape-man was making a less-than-speedy getaway to a nearby creek. Dale fired twice in its direction and then hurried inside to call the local sheriff, who employed the tried-and-true defense of laughing it off.

About a month later, Dale was watching TV around midnight when the dogs again began acting up. Shotgun in hand this time, he ran outside and followed Zipper, who appeared to be tracking something. Zipper followed the scent right into a nearby cemetery, lost the trail, then picked it up again on the other side of the graveyard. Zipper must have really been on the scent because he started running alongside the creek, barking down at the water.

Dale soon enough picked up on that awful stench and even heard something splashing in the water. He didn't claim any visual of the creature on this occasion, although he believed that the monster was only a couple of yards away. He continued tracking it into some nearby woods and then turned around. Upon arriving home, the dogs continued to act up for another hour or so.

Yet again, Dale was alerted to the presence of the creature by his dogs later that year. On this occasion, he was awakened around 4:30 in the morning by the dogs and, when he looked out the window, saw the creature moving by the creek. No doubt still thinking of the sheriff's response, he was determined to prove its existence once and for all, so grabbed his shotgun and tracked the creature back into the woods.

However, Dale wasn't only the tracker in this situation – he was also being tracked. Although Dale didn't know it, while he was chasing the beast into the woods, his mother, watching from a window, saw the creature cut back around and follow him.

The climax to these occurrences came in the spring of 1972. Both Dale and his brother had married by that point in time and were each living with their wives at the farmhouse. One evening, both the boys went out for a night on the town and left the two women at home.

When Dale and his brother arrived back, they found their wives in a hysterical state, saying that they had heard the creature trying to open the aluminum storm window. The window did exhibit tampering, though the troubling thing is that it showed no tool marks; one corner of the window had simply been pulled out, a feat that Dale believed was outside the bounds of human strength. Too, lingering around the area was the trademark rotten odor.

Two weeks later, the dogs alerted Dale to a disturbance around 11:30 p.m. He looked out the bedroom window to see the now-familiar silhouette of the beast moving along the creek, in the same direction it always moved. However, Dale must have either been too tired or too fed up to give chase and left it well enough alone.

The last documented appearance of the creature was in the fall of 1972, sometime around September. Unsurprisingly by this point, the dogs began acting up; Dale saw the creature, grabbed his shotgun, and ran after it. As usual, he was unable to get a good shot in – he claimed that, although he considered himself a pretty good shot, the creature had a particular cunning to it and was clever enough to keep far enough away from him. This last occurrence, he chased it through the cemetery and up into the woods. Although Dale waited for it to return to the cemetery, it never reappeared.

There is one final occurrence that Dale thought significant enough to mention in relation to all this strangeness. He had been out rabbit hunting in the winter of 1971 when he found a small pond dried up. Nearby, there was a thirty-foot-diameter circle of crushed weeds and grass, apparently formed in a counterclockwise swirl.

The scope of anomaly in this situation was not relegated simply to sightings of the mystery beast – but the strange thing is that the anomalies seemed to wait in line. First was simply the mysterious mist observed by Dale and his then-girlfriend, accompanied by the wave of negative feelings. Then the creature began visiting the home but, as Dale said, only when it was nice out. In the winter of 1971 he uncovered, for all intents and purposes, a crop circle next to the dried-up pond, followed by the last sightings of the creature up to September of 1972. To think that these events would be disconnected raises only more questions than answers.

One of the weirdest notions is that the creature was reported as always traveling a particular route and always the same direction. The only report where it deviates from this path was when it cut back around to follow King. This calls to mind accounts where a ghost or, regarding older folklore, a member of the fairy taxonomy haunts a particular stretch of road, always seen to travel in the same direction. This is probably best observed in cases of so-called residual haunting, where it is theorized that an image is captured and replays itself over and over through some unknown means. While the Sharpsville creature seems not to fall specifically into that category – it did, after all, react to both Zipper and King – it does seem as though this stretch of road was its designated "haunt".

Another tie to the stomping grounds of the spectral is

the inclusion of a cemetery in this case. John Keel cited cemeteries as one of the preferred stages for paranormal phenomena – and not just ghosts, but creepy creatures and flying saucers included. Researchers like Linda Godfrey, Joshua Cutchin and Timothy Renner have echoed this sentiment across their works.

The creature's behavior, described by King as appearing like it didn't know what to do, is a detail observed in other accounts of cryptids, including the infamous dogman and Bigfoot. This ineptitude was also shown in its initial smackdown with Zipper the dog, where the description of the creature swinging its punches in slow motion sounds almost glitchy.

Strangely enough is the fact that Zipper, whom King had raised since puppyhood, attacked him that initial night of the strange mist. From then on, Zipper rivaled Dale as the creature's greatest enemy, attacking or tracking it at any chance.

The creature itself was rife with bizarre attributes; one of the first to stand out is the helmetlike head described by King. As mentioned regarding Wetzel's long-armed, stiff-legged monstrosity, creature accounts often include such descriptors as "disproportionate" or "off". While this could be due to seeing an as-of-yet unknown animal, the odd proportions often seem to lend a particular otherworldliness to already strange sightings. This was commented upon by King, who claimed that it looked unlike anything else on earth.

CASE 16
THE FLIGHT SUIT ENTITY

Although the night of January 19, 1972, was dark and rainy, four teenagers – John and James Yeries, Robbie Cross, and Darrell Rich – decided to go night fishing off the Battle Creek Bridge near Anderson, California. Upon nearing the area, however, their drive was interrupted by a bright, blue-white oval light crossing the road ahead of them, about a story and a half in the air. They claimed that it was so bright, it actually illuminated the interior of their vehicle.

Soon enough, they arrived at the bridge and parked the car. As soon as they exited the vehicle, they heard what John described in *The A.P.R.O. Bulletin* as a "blood-curdling scream" come from the roadside.

Upon shining their flashlight in that direction, they saw a freakish entity hunched on the ground about fifty feet away. They described the thing as a dark brown or green drab color, standing about seven feet tall with a severely hunched posture. Totally hairless, it was instead covered with lumps described by one of the boys as "like pouches in a flight suit", with one large, teardrop-shaped ear on the side of its head. When it saw the boys, it turned and ran away.

Incidentally, they had the same idea.

James and Robbie were the first to reach the car, followed closely behind by John and Darrell. The quartet jumped in the vehicle, turned the key, and – the car didn't start. It had to be pushed into action so that they could get the heck out of there.

According to the witnesses, as they left the area, they still felt as though they were being watched and chased by some presence. Out the window, they saw soundless "firecrackers" going off on the sidewalks, as well as luminous spheres of light in the fields alongside the road. These orbs came both in a blue-white color and an orange-red and moved erratically, including one particular orange ball of light shooting straight up into the sky and vanishing. Another glowing object morphed into a humanlike figure on the roadside. Strangely enough, as soon as the vehicle crossed a particular intersection, all the lights ceased.

When they reached Darrell's home, they informed his father, Dean Rich, of what had transpired. Perhaps unsurprisingly, Mr. Rich was unconvinced – he later said he thought they were "pulling his leg". Still, he returned with three out of four of the boys to the area where the sighting had occurred, pistol in hand. One of the boys refused to go back to the area.

When the three teens and Mr. Rich arrived at the location, they heard an odd, deep growl emanating from the darkness in front of them. The three initial witnesses all immediately ran back to the vehicle, Mr. Rich following close behind. Eventually, they came to the conclusion that, whatever the thing was, it was warning them away from the area. They returned to the Rich household and notified the Shasta County Sheriff's Office. A patrol car did stake out the bridge that night, but nothing further was reported. However, according to the *A.P.R.O Bulletin's* article on this case, the lump opinion of those involved was that the witnesses were being truthful.

The pouch-covered creature is odd enough – again, California's famed Sasquatch has no business here – but odd too is the particular description by one witness that it looked like "pouches in a flight suit". In conjunction with the unidentified aerial phenomena observed throughout this encounter, the connotation of a "flight suit" seems almost an attempted – key word *attempted* – stylistic tie to the skies.

The not just inclusion, but prevalence of light anomalies in this case clearly exhibits the inexorable tie between luminous phenomena and sightings of strange creatures. One of the oddest details in this case is that one of the lights was observed to form into a humanoid figure.

Throughout this book, there have been accounts of beings with luminous eyes, shiny objects, or shiny clothing. It seems that, regardless of apparent manifestation, the presence of light is one of those details that remains prevalent in entity encounters. In his book *Earth Lights*, Paul Devereux pointed out that oftentimes UFO occupants appear to be comprised of the same luminous material as their craft. He theorized that this was, perhaps, due to the entities and the craft being comprised of the same malleable energy, an energy that can somehow be enacted on by human consciousness. In this case, the formation of a humanoid figure from a light anomaly seems to exhibit that ability – however, there was also the sighting of the decidedly concrete-looking Flight Suit Creature.

Patrick Harpur in *Daimonic Reality* noted the propensity for paranormal events to have dual forms – a detailed, hard sighting, such as a craft or figure, and the more ambiguous, soft sighting of a light anomaly. John Keel picked up on this as well, theorizing that the lights may be the only objectively "true" part of paranormal phenomena, and that the more detailed appearances serve as a sort of mask. These dual forms certainly appear in this case.

One of the commonest high-strangeness aspects of paranormal encounters is the abruptness with which so many accounts begin or end. In this case, the witnesses claimed that all the phenomena ceased at the crossing of a certain intersection. Intersections or crossroads are noted by Keel in *The Mothman Prophecies* as one of a handful of locations that often play host to monster and UFO sightings, along with gravel pits, garbage dumps, and cemeteries. Crossroads are also commonly noted for their ties to spectral or occult beings and remain a mainstay of different superstitions.

Too, the initial appearance occurred near a bridge, a setting rife with symbolic and folkloric meaning. We'll cross that bridge when we get to it in Case 20, Sandown Sam.

However, one of the strangest aspects of this case has nothing to do with the bizarre pouch-covered creature or the attendant light anomalies. The key witness, Darrell Rich, is likely better known by his nickname, "the Hilltop Rapist". In the summer of 1978, Rich enacted a reign of terror in which he would rape and kill three women and a young girl; he also sexually assaulted five other women during that time frame. Rich was executed by lethal injection in March of 2000.

CASE 17

MOMO – THE MISSOURI MONSTER

Although *the* Missouri Monster scare occurred in the summer of '72, a sighting closely correlating to later accounts happened a year previous, in July of 1971. Two women – Joan Mills and Mary Ryan – were driving back to St. Louis and decided to stop along Highway 79, just north of Louisiana, Missouri, to eat a picnic lunch. Unfortunately for them, their picturesque meal was suddenly interrupted by a hideous odor, and mere moments later, the thing responsible for the stench moseyed into view.

They described it as a half-ape, half-human, hair-covered creature, standing in a nearby thicket and making strange gurgling noises. A strict departure from later encounters was the description of its face as humanlike. The two women dashed to the car, locked the doors – and realized that they had forgotten the keys.

In the purse.

On the picnic blanket.

The creature came closer to the car, gurgling all the way, and stroked the hood of the vehicle before attempting to open the door. At that point, Joan decided to lay on the horn, and the creature jumped away from the vehicle.

So, naturally, she continued blaring the horn. Unfortunately for the two frightened witnesses, the beast soon realized that the noise posed no threat. Apparently smarter than your average bear, it went over and raided their picnic – specifically devouring a peanut butter sandwich – before picking up Joan's purse, tossing it back down, and then wandering back into the woods from whence it came.

After the two women waited a moment to make sure it had actually vamoosed, one of them worked up the courage to run for the purse. They sped all the way to St. Louis, where they filed a report with the Missouri State Patrol.

Approximately one year later, on July 11, 1972, two boys, eight-year-old Terry Harrison and five-year-old Wally Harrison, were playing in their backyard at the base of Marzolf Hill, Star Hill as it's known locally. Their fifteen-year-old sister Doris was inside the home when she heard the boys scream. Upon looking out the window, she saw a hair-covered, bipedal thing about six to seven feet tall whose face couldn't be seen under a thick layer of hair.

As if that sight wasn't frightening enough, it was flecked all over with blood, presumably from the dead dog it held tucked in its arm. Coincidentally enough, a farmer reported that his new dog had vanished around that time frame. Dogs would continue to be involved in reports of the creature; after the initial sighting, the Harrison family dog became ill, including exhibiting reddened eyes and vomiting for some hours after the incident. Thankfully, it recovered after eating bread and milk.

Around the same time of this initial sighting, a woman who lived nearby reported hearing terrible growling noises.

This was just the beginning of the Harrison family's involvement with the bizarre creature, as well as other anomalies. Three days later, the children's father, Edgar Harrison, would spot two fireballs flying over Marzolf Hill. Edgar, a Pentecostal minister, had just finished up the Friday prayer meeting when he and about a dozen members of the congregation spotted the two objects – one white, the other green – which appeared to descend into some trees next to an abandoned school.

About forty-five minutes later, Edgar began hearing strange ringing noises, which he thought may be caused by the throwing of stones into a metal water reservoir at the top of Marzolf Hill. The remainder of his family insisted that they leave the area immediately.

Two police officers were called to the scene but found nothing out of the ordinary. It was after they left that Edgar would encounter the infamous stench for the first time and assembled a small posse to go investigate on the hill. They came upon an old building that emitted an odor that Edgar described as akin to "moldy horse or strong garbage"; Edgar would later realize that this odor would accompany areas with strange noises.

And there was certainly a plethora of unexplainable

sounds in the area. Reports came in of odd growls, a woman screaming, and a baby crying; interestingly enough, the latter two, particularly the phantom screams, had long haunted the Louisiana area. Also, strangely enough, several cases of disembodied voices were heard in this area.

On the twenty-ninth of July, Harrison and a group of students heard the voice of an old man come from a small patch of trees. It said, "You boys stay out of those woods." A search revealed no such old man – as a matter of fact, it revealed no one at all. Another disembodied voice occurred on August 5, when two friends were sitting in the Harrison backyard, drinking coffee. This time, a voice purportedly said, "I'll take a cup of your coffee." No source for the voice could be found.

The creature would continue to plague the Harrison family so badly that Mrs. Harrison and the kids actually lived out of the restaurant they managed in town, never to return to the home. Edgar, on the other hand, devoted himself to solving the mystery. Strangely enough, he would never actually get a visual of the creature.

However, the Harrisons weren't the only ones plagued by the hairy hominid. Reports came in from around the area of dark-haired, bipedal things, including the account of Ellis Minor. On July 21, at around 10:00 in the evening, Minor's dog began growling. Upon shining a flashlight outside, he glimpsed a six-foot-tall, hair-covered creature. When the light hit it, it retreated into the woods.

On the nineteenth, a posse of twenty people, including

Edgar and Police Chief Shelby Ward, marched over Marzolf Hill in an attempt to flush out the creature. Nothing was found.

The next day, Edgar returned to Marzolf Hill, joined by his daughter's boyfriend Richard Bliss, *Fate* magazine and Chicago *Irish Times* reporter Richard Crowe, and investigator Loren Smith. Although the creature itself would remain elusive, several odd facts were soon unearthed.

First of all was a circular spot of brush that appeared to have been cleared of leaves and twigs. Second, something had been digging through a nearby garbage dump, and finally, two dog graves had been opened, their bones scattered throughout the area.

As the four men neared an abandoned shack, the Harrison family dog ran away. No sooner did it run off than the men were assailed by the overwhelming stench of rotten flesh or foul water. Despite a thorough search, nothing was seen. In the distance, all the neighborhood dogs could be heard yapping.

Two tracks were recovered by the intrepid posse – one of a foot, the other a curved impression of a hand. However, further analysis by the director of the Oklahoma City Zoo concluded that the prints were made by something like a snow mitten or dish glove. Sightings of the creature would continue with regularity through August before tapering off, though accounts still come in of similar Sasquatch-like creatures to this day.

Momo raises a question I usually reserve for UFO flaps

– why did the phenomenon heighten *then*? It seems that there are certain places more prone to paranormal phenomena than others and that, for whatever reason, they sometimes flare up, experiencing flaps of intense activity that then die down into the more normal scope.

The takeaway from the Missouri Monster flap is that the area around Louisiana, Missouri, already had a reputation as a haunted area, prone to spook lights and spectral screams. This was the stage set for an increase in that activity, plus the appearance of a strange, stinky, apelike being.

At the time of the Missouri Monster scare, some of the first investigators at the scene were MUFON field investigators. Because of this, and in conjunction with the white and green fireballs observed in the area, one of the most popular theories for the creature was that it was some sort of extraterrestrial entity.

One of Momo's more negative connotations became apparent in the first of the Harrison sightings when it was carrying a dead dog under its arm. The fact that the dog burial sites had been scattered only adds to this eerie canine connotation. Dogs repeatedly set themselves up as adversaries to anomalies – alarming their masters to disturbances, sometimes even tracking said disturbances, other times cowering away. Dogs have often been seen to vanish in the face of the unknown – such as one of the great kickoffs to the events of *The Mothman Prophecies*, the disappearance of Merle Partridge's dog Bandit.

In looking at cases such as Momo, where an apparently physical creature is observed carrying a dead dog, the practical reason is obvious – wrong place, wrong time. To take a step onto the rickety pier of conjecture and look at the symbolic reason for this, especially in the wider scope of dogs and their relation to paranormal phenomena, is this repeated action a symbol of the destruction of loyalty and guardianship in the face of the unknown?

CASE 18
RORO – THE ROACHDALE CREATURE

Occurring in the same time frame as good ol' Momo and bearing many similarities to that far more infamous case is the creature of Roachdale, Indiana, here affectionately referred to as – drumroll, please – Roro.

Sometime in August of 1972, in the farmland surrounding Roachdale, Indiana, a man was visiting at a farmhouse when he saw a luminous object over a neighboring cornfield. The object hovered for a moment and then promptly blew up. The man was shaken, thinking that he had just watched a plane explode, but upon closer examination there was no wreckage in the fields. Whatever it was left no trace – unless you count the near spectral, Bigfoot-like creature that came to haunt the Roachdale area.

Coincidentally enough, the man's sister, Lou Rogers, would become one of the leading witnesses in this particular case, and in short order. About half an hour after the luminous object exploded, Lou and her young son Keith had just stepped out of their rented farmhouse to roll up the windows on the family car. Dark was drawing on, and a light drizzle had just settled over the evening. As they stepped out into the yard, both Lou and Keith heard a growling-type sound described as "boo" or "oo" – and thought nothing of it. At first.

When it happened a second time, Lou got the impression that the sound hadn't come from an animal, but a person. Keith became very upset at this time, and Lou then felt something breathe down the back of her neck. When she turned to face them, no one was there.

The two promptly ran inside.

However, this was just the beginning of a fiasco in which an anomalous, part-poltergeist part-Sasquatch creature would leave far more than footprints. The Rogers' house began to be plagued by the disconcerting noises of someone pounding on the siding and windows, each night becoming progressively louder. Strangely enough, these noises kept a regular schedule, with Lou claiming that they would occur between the hours of ten and eleven thirty every night. Not only were the Rogers treated to this nightly percussive performance, but the creature also emanated a strong perfume of garbage or rotten flesh.

Lou's husband, Randy, was so concerned for his family's safety that he even borrowed his father's shotgun. When the noises started up, he'd run outside to confront whoever – or whatever – it was that was so intent on disrupting his family's peace. Though he never claimed to have shot the beast, he did see it, describing it as a broad-shouldered, bipedal, hairy thing about six feet tall. The family also stated that, although it would stand on two feet, it would typically run off on all fours.

Once, over the course of the two-to-three-week-long harassment by the mystery thing, it even bobbed up and down outside the windows, peering in at Lou as she washed dishes.

The couple also didn't leave the debunking up to the Air Force – at first, they figured it must be a gorilla. However, barring the typical lack of usual suspects – no zoo escapees or renegade circus animals were in the area at the time – this theory was pretty thoroughly demolished by a few of the creature's stranger habits. Including the fact that it often appeared to be translucent.

This was hardly the only strange thing about the creature. The family also stated that it was absolutely sound-less while running away, leaving no tracks in the muddy areas through which it walked.

The creature was so persistent that Randy even organized a small posse to try to capture the thing. Surprisingly enough, one among the group was lucky – or unlucky – enough to spot it stepping out of a ditch. He called out a warning, which, needless to say, the creature didn't abide. Ends up, it didn't need to.

The man shot at the animal to absolutely no effect.

The Rogers family members were not the only people beset by strange phenomena at this time. All told, about fifty people would come forward throughout the summer to report their sightings. On the fourteenth of August, a woman, her husband, and daughter reported that two "balls of fire" across the road had stared at them for the better part of the night.

This is a strange report – the witness kept referring to the objects simply as balls of fire, yet phrased their behavior as that of eyes, without directly stating there was an entity that the eyes belonged to.

She claimed that, eventually, the first pair of eyes was joined by another one. Every now and again they would turn from staring at the family to watch a passing car, then turn back. Eventually, the father and daughter went to bed, leaving the woman to watch the strange things from the window. She said that every now and again the eyes would drop on all fours, feeding like a dog, before popping back up again. She watched the eyes watch her for hours, finally retiring to bed at around 3:40 in the morning. The eyes were still there.

The climax of this monster scare was the chaos that befell the Burdine family on August 22. At nine o'clock, Carter Burdine and his uncle, Junior, came home to discover the remains of about sixty chickens ripped apart and scattered in a path of the utmost "fowl" carnage imaginable.

Oddly enough, the chickens had not been eaten, simply shredded apart and spread out in a path that spanned the area between the coop and the front yard, about two hundred feet.

The Burdines called the town marshal, Leroy Clones.

As they were standing around discussing the matter, they heard a noise between the chicken coop and the road. The marshal got in his car while Junior followed him on foot. Without warning, some indeterminate thing jumped up out of the ditch and ran across the road six feet ahead of Junior, but behind the car. Junior was so startled, he didn't have time to get a good look at it, let alone fire his weapon.

Strangely enough, considering that the Rogers had claimed that the creature moved soundlessly, left no tracks, and seemed not to touch its surroundings, this account claims the opposite. The thing trampled a fence, leaving a trail of crushed weeds and grass in its wake. Carter Burdine also claims that he distinctly heard the sound of some bipedal thing running. Also at this time, there was a musty odor in the area, and the Burdines' "meanest dog" was found cowering up against the porch. Their other dog had hidden in its pen.

At this point, Carter remembered that the night before, he had heard something heavy moving around on the porch.

This was by no means the last time that the creature would come calling at the Burdine household. Some hours later, Carter and Junior had just arrived back at the farm after dropping Carter's wife off at some relatives' in town. By the time they arrived back at the farmhouse, it was early morning. As they pulled up to the farm, they saw the creature standing in the chicken house door. The door's dimensions were six by eight feet, and both men claimed that the creature totally blocked out the lights inside the chicken house.

Now, the two men were able to get a good look at the creature, claiming that it was covered in long, rust-colored hair, which obscured the face, and made a sound described by Junior as a "groaning racket".

The thing ran into the barn and jumped into a haymow. Carter, now joined by his father Herman, approached the building, firearms at the ready, while Junior went around the side. Suddenly, Junior yelled, "Bring me a light."

By the time Carter and Herman rejoined Junior, he was already busy firing at something loping across the field. He claimed that the thing was only a hundred feet away and that he, by all accounts an avid rabbit hunter, was certain that he hit it. Although Herman couldn't see anything, he also joined in shooting in the monster's general direction. As with so many cryptid accounts, the creature simply kept walking, apparently unbothered by the shower of bullets.

Strangely enough, the witnesses claimed that as it retreated, it was soundless and left no tracks in the field. What it did leave behind were the strewn, bloodless remains of one hundred ten chickens. The Burdines had entered this strange tale with two hundred chickens and were then down to thirty. Cases would subside over the next week before Roro finally disappeared into wherever it is these strange creatures usually do.

The parallels to the more infamous Missouri Monster

are evident. Roro was preceded by a luminous object in the sky – Momo was attended by white and green fireballs. Both creatures possessed a terrible odor, and both appeared more violent than your average Bigfoot; Momo appeared carrying a dead, blood-flecked dog, and Roro was held responsible for the slaughter of over 150 chickens. Both creatures were also associated with disembodied voices.

The beating on the house in this case calls to mind poltergeist manifestations, known for their violent beating on walls and other surfaces. Roro itself also appeared nearly spectral for the multiple accounts that described it as "translucent" or "like you could see right through it".

The translucency, in combination with physical effects, is intriguing, and the whole sequence of events points to something of a transient nature. In line with many other entity encounters, the Roachdale beast was preceded by a light anomaly. The disembodied voice was the next disturbance; early sightings of the creature pegged it as appearing translucent and nonphysical, being sound-less and leaving no tracks in the muddy ground through which it walked. However, as time went on, it seemed to gain physicality, beginning with the beating on the house, the flattening of the fence, and climaxing with the slaughter of the chickens.

However, when it was pursued after this climax, it once again appeared nonphysical, impervious to gunfire, soundless and, once again, left no tracks. This is the phenomenological crossroads of paranormal experience –

something that must be both physical and nonphysical, a true paradox. Roro was capable of physical effects – the 170 dead chickens and flattened fence are a testament to that – but must also have been capable of immateriality, as the bullets appeared not just ineffectual, but as if they had zero effect, plus the lack of tracks through muddy ground.

Dead livestock, particularly of the bloodless variety, are a mainstay of UFO lore, yet here they are showing up in direct connection with what we would conventionally term a mystery primate. Of course, this mystery primate was also observed in conjunction with an exploding light anomaly; and said primate exhibited classic behaviors associated with poltergeist manifestations. Whatever Roro was and wherever it wandered off to, the disturbances associated with it are a prime example of cross-genre phenomena.

CASE 19

THE ENFIELD HORROR

There are some cases so strange, they are best labelled, to use Keel's term, "the incomprehensibles". The Enfield Horror is one of them.

Mr. and Mrs. McDaniel of Enfield, Illinois, returned to their home the evening of April 25, 1973 to find their children, Henry Jr. and Lil, in a panic. The two kids had been watching TV when they heard a scratching at the door and, like any sensible youngsters home alone, didn't answer it. Then the scratching moved to the air-conditioning unit perched in their window.

As if on cue, as the kids were telling their parents about the dreadful event, the scratching started up again at the door.

Mr. McDaniel, expecting to come face-to-snot-nosed-face with a teenaged prankster, instead was greeted by what he first thought was just, according to multiple newspaper articles, "some animal". Still, he turned back into the house and grabbed his .22 pistol and a flashlight. When he returned to the doorway and shined his flashlight on the creature, he realized that it was something else entirely.

What McDaniel first noticed were big, pink eyes that reminded him of reflectors. These were set in a large head atop a nearly humanoid body. The being stood between four and five feet tall. Two short, taloned arms jutted out of its chest, and the whole thing was covered in gray hair. However, the defining characteristic of this creepy-crawly creature was the fact that it stood on no less than three legs.

McDaniel immediately shot at the creature four times – considering it stood on his front porch, about three feet away, he was certain that he hit it at least once. Instead of succumbing to its injuries, the creature merely let out a loud hiss and bounded out into the night, disappearing down some railroad tracks. McDaniel claimed that it covered about seventy-five feet in only three jumps.

Although the McDaniel encounter is likely the most infamous sighting of the strange, three-legged wonder, it was by no means the closest encounter. That distinction goes to a ten-year-old neighbor boy, Greg Garrett. Garrett had gone outside to feed his dogs when a bizarre creature jumped on his foot. Garrett ran inside screaming; his uncle claimed that he was hysterical following the sighting. Garrett later described the beast as identical to the one reported by McDaniel.

The police and Illinois state troopers were called in regarding these incidents, curiosity seekers and monster hunters abounded, and sightings continued. A group of five hunters even claimed to have opened fire on the creature, which appeared unaffected. Incidentally, these five men were charged with hunting violations, as according to Greenfield, Indiana's *The Daily Reporter* article, Deputy County Sheriff Clark said, "Nothing I know of is in season now, especially monsters."

Rick Rainbow, a news director from WWKI in Kokomo, Indiana, recorded a high-pitched screeching noise and even claimed a visual sighting of the creature in an abandoned barn. Even famed cryptozoologist Loren Coleman, who was on the scene to investigate the beastie, heard an anomalous scream.

On May 6, Mr. McDaniel was awakened out of his slumber around 3:00 in the morning by all the neighborhood dogs raising a ruckus. He looked out the window to see the creature lumbering along the railroad tracks before, again, bouncing off into the night.

All this bouncing led to a popular theory – was the creature an escaped kangaroo? A letter addressed to the Enfield newspaper from one Alan Yorkshire of Elyria, Ohio, claimed that Mr. Yorkshire had a pet kangaroo, which had been stolen about a year previous.

As to why it took a year for the 'roo to bounce through Enfield, there was no comment. Nor was the $500 reward offered by Mr. Yorkshire ever claimed, as the strange creature seems to have decided it was finally time to bounce.

The biggest problem with the kangaroo theory is this; in his younger days, while serving with the army in Australia, McDaniel himself became familiar with kangaroos. As a matter of fact, he even kept one as a pet for a time. In addition to the fact that he was adamant the creature he saw was no wayward marsupial, he shot it at near point-blank range. The thing simply bounded off, unharmed, and was later able to survive another round of gunfire by the hunters apprehended by local police.

And as suddenly as it appeared, the creature was gone.

The screams that plagued the area, and were recorded by Rick Rainbow, are yet another classic example of spectral screams accompanying weird critters. In this case, however, the critter in question is *exceptionally* weird.

The Enfield Horror, to the best of my knowledge, stands alone on its three legs. It bounced through Enfield and then on to wherever the heck these things usually do. This flies in the face of cryptozoology in the true sense of the word: the study of hidden animals. The flesh-and-blood hypothesis dictates that, for a creature to exist, it must be one of a breeding population, and that this population must be sustained. In the case of the Enfield Horror, barring theories of some genetic mutant running wild in Illinois, the flesh-and-blood explanation leaves a lot to be desired.

So if not the flesh-and-blood explanation, what then?

Across his work, Keel postulated that these strange beings may not be solely physical, but rather, transient forms he referred to as "transmogrifications of energy". Given the description rampant across so many encounters with strange beings that something seemed "off" about the entity, this seems to be evidence that the image is malleable and may sometimes get lost in translation – or rather, lost in transmogrification. The Enfield Horror is a posterchild of a concept I have termed "flopped projections". Many paranormal entities seem to fall into certain patterns – Bigfoot, dogman, the great taxonomy of extraterrestrials, etc. – and then there's the Enfield horror, a real three-legged fly in the ointment.

Speculating symbolically, I find it of interest that two of the main appearances of the creature – the initial McDaniel encounter and the sighting by Rick Rainbow – placed the creature in a doorway. McDaniel saw the creature standing just outside his porch door, whereas Rainbow saw it in the doorway of an abandoned barn. Doorways are one of the classic liminal points, and there are countless superstitions regarding the dwelling of spirits on this threshold; one infamous example of this is the lying across the threshold of the Barghest, one of many traditional black spectral dogs of the British Isles. Incidentally, and bearing a relationship to the Enfield Horror, the Barghest was said to have glowing eyes.

CASE 20
SANDOWN SAM

Regarding this next case, I still don't know how to answer the *BUFORA Journal*'s coy question, "Report – Extra! Ghost or Spaceman '73?"

One Tuesday afternoon in May of 1973, a seven-year-old girl pseudonymously referred to as Fay and an unnamed boy of around the same age were walking near Lake Common, Sandown, on the Isle of Wight, England, when they heard a strange noise that they compared to an ambulance siren or an odd wailing. More curious than cautious, they decided to follow the noise across a golf course and through a hedge into a swampy meadow near the Sandown Airport. When they hit the meadow, the noise stopped.

They were crossing a brook on a little wooden footbridge when a hand in a blue glove popped out from under the bridge, followed by a truly odd creature. They described the being – which will, like good ol' Flix, name itself later in the encounter – as standing about seven feet tall. It had, much like many hairy humanoid reports, no discernable neck, rather the head sat firmly in the shoulders. However, unlike most hairy humanoid reports, this thing was not, in fact, covered in hair, but, in addition to the blue gloves, wore a tattered, nearly Pied Piper-like getup: white pants, a green tunic with a red collar, and a yellow, pointed hood, which seemed to be attached to the collar. The being had three fingers each on each blue-gloved hands, and three toes on each bare foot.

This entity had a flat, round, white face with triangles for eyes, a square for the nose, and unmoving yellow lips. Each cheek bore a round mark, and a red fringe of hair lay across its forehead. To top it all off, a black "knob" protruded from the top of its hood, and on either side of his face were wooden antennae. Wooden slats also protruded from the sleeves and pant legs.

Now, when the being first emerged from under the bridge, it was holding a book, which it dropped into the water, retrieved, and then "hopped" along to a windowless metal "hut" nearby.

Interestingly enough, the two children weren't much enthused about this bizarre creature. Initially, they felt no fear, concern, or curiosity. As a matter of fact, they just continued to wander along much as they had been doing. When they were about fifty yards away, the thing showed up near the metal hut, this time with a microphone. The wailing noise started up and frightened the boy, who began running away – infinitely more sensible than most –

however, at that point, the thing spoke into the microphone, and its voice showed up right next to the children. It said, "Hello, are you still there?" in such a friendly voice that Fay and her friend decided to go over to it. As they drew closer, it decided to use a different medium to communicate – a notebook. The creature wrote out a jumble of words and then pointed to each word in order, which Fay spoke out loud.

The message read, "Hello, and I am all colours, Sam."

As the children moved closer, "Sam" began speaking without the use of the microphone or notebook; however, the lips were never seen to move.

The first question the children asked Sam was why his clothing was all ripped.

He replied that it was his only set, not bothering to explain what, exactly, had happened. Then they ventured to ask if he was really a man, to which Sam replied, "No."

Their next, rather logical question was if Sam was a ghost.

Sam said, "Well, not really, but I am in an odd sort of way."

They then asked what he really was, to which Sam replied, "You know."

After christening himself Sam, the being then went on to claim that he had no name, there were more things like him, and that he was scared of people.

At this point, the tale goes from the bizarre to the downright disturbing. Sam invited the kids into his nearby hut, which they had to crawl through a flap to enter. Inside were two stories – the lower one was downright homey, with wooden furniture, an electric heater, and blue-green wallpaper, which had a dial pattern on it. The upper floor was smaller with a metallic floor.

Once inside, Sam told the kids a variety of things, such as the fact that he had an additional "camp" on the mainland, and that he could clean the river water to drink it. He also took off his hood, and the children saw that he had round, white ears and thin brown hair, which doesn't explain the fringe of red hair on his forehead.

Sam also told them that he ate berries, which he gathered in the late afternoons, and showed them, presumably, how he ingested them. He put a berry in his ear and nodded his head forward. The berry vanished from the ear and then reappeared at one of his eyes. He did this once more, and the berry ended up in his mouth.

The children talked with Sam for around a half hour and then, after saying their goodbyes, ran to tell the nearest adult that they'd seen a ghost. Said first adult was a workman, who just laughed at them.

Apparently, the children came to the conclusion that it was either a ghost or someone dressed up. Among other things, Fay claimed that the whole time, there were two workmen nearby repairing a post – they seemed to take no notice of the creepy figure or the fact that two young children accompanied the figure to a hut.

Unfortunately, Fay didn't bother to tell her father about the sighting until early June. Even so, Mr. Y also claims that he returned to the area to look for the metal shed to no avail – unfortunately, as this was three weeks after the incident, it's within the bounds of possibility that a shed could have been moved.

As bizarre as Fay's experience was, her father, Mr. Y, seems to have had a knack for anomalies, which, according to the *BUFORA Journal*, started in October of 1970. While driving from the town of Shanklin, Mr. Y passed through the village of Brading when he became aware of a multi-lit "aircraft" flying low over the nearby swamps.

He stopped his vehicle and watched as the object continued over the river Yar. He said it looked like a wide ring of approximately seven bright, large, spherical lights, which Mr. Y said each looked "like a bright red cherry", interspersed by turquoise and white lights. The whole thing was absolutely soundless.

He continued on his way, and the object did as well, soaring parallel to his vehicle until it maneuvered across the road and dropped behind him, then moved aimlessly and slowly while reducing in apparent size. The number of lights decreased to four, and these rotated slowly. Mr. Y actually beckoned to the thing with his flashlight for ten minutes, and for that duration it moved back and forth. I guess getting bored with this anomaly in the sky, he continued on his way to his friend's house. When they both came outside, the lights were still there, moving behind the treetops. Eventually, they were lost to view.

Over the next couple of years, Mr. Y would see single balls of red light, claiming that they would sometimes follow him along, while other times they were stationary.

However, a far more dramatic occurrence happened in March of 1972, a little over a year before his daughter's infamous experience.

Between 9:00 and 10:00 in the evening, Mr. Y was sitting on a cliff at Compton Bay when he saw two points of yellow light, which he referred to as "eyes", about forty feet away, glaring up at him from just below the surface of the water.

The inclusion of Fay's father's cases, however, definitely add some intrigue here. Although neither account was as close or dramatic as Sam the clown-thing, the case of the red lights stands out because they appeared to be tailing him, and it was after this sighting that he began seeing these lights on what sounds like a near-regular basis. In addition, while his sighting of the thing in the ocean was investigated in a strictly ufological sense, we can't get away from the fact that he referred to those two points of light beneath the waves as eyes, calling to mind the form of some great beast lurking just offshore.

It's not too much of a leap to suggest that, for whatever reason, the initial sighting of the red lights began an entanglement of Mr. Y with these anomalies, which continued largely in light form until escalating to something indicative of a giant monster in the waves. Finally, it culminated with the infamous sighting of Sam.

Sam is a difficult figure to pin down; the children's final statement that it was, take your pick, a guy in a costume or a ghost, doesn't give us much to go off of. I will say that, if Sam was indeed a man in a clown suit, this makes his motivations for a very different type of abduction far more sinister than a quick visit to the otherworld via metallic hut.

However, I find it odd that the two workmen near the sighting wouldn't have taken some interest in, again, a guy in a clown suit talking to two children. Heck, even if he wasn't talking to two children, I find it odd they wouldn't take an interest. In combination with Fay's father's earlier encounters, I find it possible that Sam was anomalous.

This one series of encounters – Fay's and her father's – exhibit a behavior that I've noticed across many accounts. It seems as though cases of contact are ushered in by a light anomaly or odd noise. In different scopes, this case has both. Mr. Y's earlier encounters were of lights in the sky – it can be argued that these escalated into the encounter with Sam. Fay's particular encounter began with the odd wailing noise, which seemed to nearly "lure" her and her friend into the area where they would find Sam.

The encounter with Sam himself appears highly symbolic in nature. The fact that the children were crossing a bridge calls to mind other accounts of waterways, symbolically associated with the unconscious mind. Sam's initial position of lurking under the bridge immediately reminds me of "The Three Billy Goats Gruff", which of course features a troll underneath the bridge. Bridges have a long-standing history of being associated with different paranormal or folkloric beliefs. Serving as a symbol of liminality between two worlds, they often claim spectral manifestations, demons, fairies, even the Black Shuck.

Sam's appearance as, for all intents and purposes, nearly clown-like seems perfectly fit to his young audience. Although so-called coulrophobia, the unofficial moniker for a fear of clowns, is common enough (at the time of this writing, the count is one out of every ten adults), there's no denying an iconographical connection between clowns and young children. In combination with his insistence that he was afraid of people, it really does seem as though Sam was geared towards appearing harmless to the children.

The displacement of Sam's voice, as well as his method of speaking without moving his mouth, is reminiscent of apparitional appearances where an apparition is seen and a voice is heard – but the face of the spook doesn't move. Oftentimes, too, the voice is heard directly next to the witness, just as Sam's voice did in this account.

While on the topic, I'm going to mention a very small aspect of this case – the berry. The conjuring trick of tossing it around in his noggin is reminiscent of accounts where UFO-related entities or even the MIB perform small, yet impressive feats of magic, as though to prove that they are every bit as inhuman as they claim to be. In addition to that, the inclusion of a berry in such a prominent way is odd to me because of their connections to the Fairy Faith. There are numerous taboos throughout the Celtic Fairy Faith regarding picking berries at certain times of year, or in certain places – the siren-like sound associated with Sam also calls to mind the otherworldly music of the Good Folk, often compared to piping noise. Oddly enough, berry-picking makes its random appearance in the Missing 411 works of David Paulides, making me wonder if the two children had stayed longer in the cozy, wallpapered hut, they may never have turned up again.

CASE 21

THE PASCAGOULA ABDUCTION

Around 8:00 in the evening of October 11, 1973, the lives of two men were about to be dramatically changed. Forty-two-year-old Charles Hickson and his friend, eighteen-year-old Calvin Parker, were fishing off a pier on the Pascagoula River in the town of Pascagoula, Missouri. Coworkers at a local shipyard, the two were simply enjoying the evening when they heard a loud pulsing, humming sound. Noted by John Keel in *The Eighth Tower*, the Pascagoula is actually nicknamed "the singing river" due to a mysterious, flutelike noise that has been heard to emanate from the river for centuries. Although no explanation has been forthcoming for this pleasant oddity, local legends chalk it up to a mermaid – I'll let the reader take that as they will.

The two men then saw a brilliant, flickering blue light moving over the water in their direction. Suddenly, it came to a stop, hovering about eight feet over a scattering of rock and gravel belonging to an old auto-wrecking yard. At this point, they described the object as football-shaped, about thirty feet long and ten feet high, topped with a dome-like structure.

The blue light went out, and an opening appeared in the craft, immediately populated by three entities. Both men described them as being about five feet tall and humanoid in the loosest sense of the term. They had no neck, their heads morphing directly into the shoulders, and were totally covered in wrinkly gray skin. According to Hickson, their faces were too wrinkly to determine if they had eyes or not, though they did have a slit for a mouth and a pointed nose about two inches long. On each side of the head were "ears", which looked exactly like the nose. Their disproportionately long arms terminated in mitten or crab-like claws, and Hickson described their feet as looking elephant-like.

The strange entities "floated" out of the craft and down the twenty yards of the pier to Hickson and Parker, who were struck senseless by the sighting. Two entities grabbed Hickson by the arms, while a third took Parker, whom Hickson claimed had fallen into a faint.

Hickson said that when they first made physical contact with his arms, there was a pain in his left arm that evaporated. Immediately thereafter, he became paralyzed and unable to feel. He claimed the inside of the object was blindingly bright, and that he was unable to close his eyes. While in this state, a basketball-sized eye moved over Hickson's body. When this was through, Hickson was again picked up by two entities, floated out of the opening, and deposited back on the pier. By his recollection, Parker was still standing there.

Parker would later recall, through the use of regression hypnosis, being taken on board the craft as well, and experienced many aspects now well associated with the alien abduction phenomenon, including being taken into a bright room with no visible light source and laid on a sloping table.

Parker heard a clicking noise, which he claimed came from a blue box about the size of a deck of cards. After hearing this, a smaller entity entered the room. As in many reports of alien abduction, Parker associated this entity as being far more positive than his initial captors, even claiming that it made him feel safe.

In contrast to the eyeless, wrinkly beings first observed, he claimed that this being had large brown eyes and said that it was "pleasant looking" in comparison to the other entities. Parker also credited this entity with saying the phrase "don't be afraid" at one point in his encounter, but without moving its lips.

The same buzzing noise ensued, there was a blue flash of light, and the craft was gone. The whole experience allegedly took between thirty and forty minutes.

Strangely enough, when the two men went for Parker's car, the windows on one side were reportedly shattered, and the vehicle took several tries to start.

Hickson and Parker contacted the sheriff, who, after questioning them thoroughly, also hid a secret tape recorder in a room as the two men conversed "privately". Instead of congratulating each other on a well-executed hoax, the tape recorder actually picked up both men discussing the details of the event, as well as their emotional distress.

Not only was there an initial police investigation, but there was also a brief initial attempt at hypnotic regression attempted by an engineering professor from Berkeley. However, the session was cut short when the men began acting out in terror – the professor's opinion was that they had been captured by outer-space robots.

According to Hickson's account, the first authority he had turned to was none other than Keesler Air Force Base. However, they recommended calling the local police, with a bizarre PS that the US Air Force was no longer inter-ested in UFOs. Someone apparently didn't get the memo.

Shortly afterward, however, an Air Force investigation ensued. The two witnesses, in the company of Deputy Tom Huntley, arrived at the base with a police escort. After being welcomed by masked, gloved scientists, Hickson and Parker were treated to a physical examina-tion, radioactivity check, and an interrogation viewed by the top brass as well as a panel of doctors. Strangely enough, many questions asked of the men were on diet, family history, and bodily wounds.

After the event, both men experienced headaches and nightmares in addition to other bizarre effects. Hickson had a small wound mysteriously open up and bleed, then just as mysteriously close up. Parker suffered two nervous breakdowns from the incident, and it's just recently that he has decided to come forward publicly about the encounter.

On the other hand, Hickson was very forthcoming about his experience at the time, best summed up in the first words of his police interview.

"Even though I'll be the laughingstock of the country, I'll tell what I've seen and the experiences I've had."

After this initial experience, Hickson seemed to gather UFO sightings. In an interview with UFO researcher Ray Stanford in the August 1978 edition of *UFO Report,* Stanford brought up the fact that Hickson was rumored to have been "followed" by UFOs after the Pascagoula sighting. This rumor was only strengthened when a UFO showed up in the presence of Hickson at Stanford's Project Starlight International.

Also, it was claimed by Hickson that, following his experience, he was unable to wear a watch. No matter what brand, they would either keep incorrect time or stop altogether.

There were other accounts from the area at the time. Slightly over thirty miles away from Pascagoula is the small town of Tanner Williams, Alabama. On October 11 of 1973, a three-year-old boy informed his mother that he had been playing with "some old monster" in their backyard. When pressed for details, he claimed that it had pointed ears and was covered with wrinkly gray skin.

Some weeks afterward, on November 8, the *Cincinnati Post* reported that a man named Raymond Ryan, his son, and Raymond's twin brother, Rayme, had observed a mysterious object while fishing on the Pascagoula the previous Tuesday. Raymond claimed that an underwater light had followed his boat. He described the light as being parachute-shaped and about nine feet in diameter, bright enough to shine a milky white above the surface of the water. In spite of his best attempts to get rid of it – his best attempts being smacking the light with an oar – the light merely dimmed. Finally, it moved off toward deeper water in a move that Raymond felt was evasive – maybe the oar had actually worked.

Raymond didn't plan to tell anyone about his sighting, but finally relayed it to his twin brother. The two men went back out, managed to find the light, and attempted to poke it with oars again.

When this great plan didn't effect any change on the object, they decided to get the Coast Guard involved. The Coast Guard sent out a boat to find the object. When located, the object was described as a bright metal object with an amber beam, only about four to five inches in diameter. It was moving at a speed of four to six knots in about four to six feet of water, maneuvering along various courses. Attempts to retrieve the object failed, as it would appear to extinguish and then reappear in a different spot.

The Pascagoula Encounter presents some of the problems rife with the purely physical theory of alien abductions. One of the first problems is the fact that Hickson observed that Parker passed out – Parker later claimed that he too had been taken on board the craft. This isn't proof that either of the men was lying – but it points to the concept that the abduction at Pascagoula was not a physical abduction – but that's not to say that it was purely hallucinatory. Something strange had descended in the Pascagoula area, including the sighting of "some old monster" that suspiciously resembled Hickson and Parker's visitors, as well as the bizarre luminous object observed in the Pascagoula River some weeks later.

Hynek, who investigated the Pascagoula Abduction and spoke to the two witnesses, struggled with this dichotomy, noting that there was no physical evidence that a craft had landed – but that both men were sincere in their telling of the experience. In *The Edge of Reality*, he postulates the notion that the Pascagoula abduction was more in line with "a religious experience, as if they had seen the Virgin Mary".

CASE 22

DOVER DEMON

In April of 1977, the small town of Dover, Massachusetts, was beset by its very own demon...at least, that's what the name suggests.

The first account came on April 21 from seventeen-year-old William Bartlett. Although he was accompanied by two friends as he drove through town around 10:00 that night, neither would see the bizarre creature. Off to the side of the road, moseying near a low stone wall, was what Bill thought was a cat or dog. However, as so very many of these accounts detail, it was hardly a furry friend at all.

Instead, it was a hairless being with a bulbous, watermelon-sized head set on a thin neck. Its torso was about the same size as the head, and it had long, spindly arms and legs. Its furless skin appeared, as recorded in Walter Webb's fantastic report printed in Loren Coleman's *Mysterious America*, "like wet sandpaper" and was an "exaggerated skin color, like Fred Flintstone in the Sunday comics". It had large, orange, lidless eyes. The whole creature stood only about three and a half feet tall.

Bill sped away, asking his friends if they had seen the creature. They hadn't and begged him to turn around. Bill, deeply upset by this odd sighting, finally was convinced to do so. By the time he returned to the area, the creature had vanished.

About two hours later, fifteen-year-old John Baxter was walking home from his girlfriend's house a little over a mile away from Bartlett's sighting. About a hundred feet ahead of him, he saw what he thought was the silhouette of a child approaching him. Thinking it was a young acquaintance who lived nearby, he even called out to it and received no response. Both the silhouette and the witness continued walking closer until finally the figure stopped when it was between fifteen and twenty-five feet away. The witness demanded to know who it was, and it was at this point that the figure quickly ran to the left into a gully and up a bank.

John ran after the creature, then stopped as he saw it standing on a rock, with its feet gripping the rock and its long-fingered hands wrapped around a small tree trunk. Silhouetted against the open field behind it, the creature appeared to have a large head, the eyes visible as two light spots in the center of the face. After remaining deadlocked in a stare-off with the creature, John became unnerved and decided to quickly continue on his way.

The last sighting would occur near midnight of the

following day. Eighteen-year-old Will Taintor was driving fifteen-year-old Abby Brabham from Dover to her home in Sherborn. Just outside Dover, Abby claimed to see a large, oblong-headed, hairless creature crouched along the road-side. She claimed that the creature was beige/tan and hair-less. In line with the other sightings, she saw no mouth, nose, ears, or tail; however, in contrast to the other sight-ings, she maintained that the eyes glowed bright green. By the time Will noticed the thing, all he got was a passing glance of the creature.

Like the Enfield Horror, the Dover Demon is not a practical member of the animal kingdom. Lacking mouth or nose, there have also been no repeat sightings indicative of a breeding population.

But here's the problem – it was still spotted. And not just by one individual, but by four, with the confirmation of Bill's emotional state by two of his friends.

As discussed in earlier chapters, faceless beings are rife throughout the annals of paranormal lore. This case details another common being lacking in the feature department – countless cases detail creatures whose only noticeable feature is their usually prominent eyes. As noted in the Shrum Encounter, this is also observed in conjunction with UFO-related entities. The importance of eyes in these encounters can also be seen in the prominent eyes of one of UFO lore's most infamous denizens, the Grays. However, in the Dover case, there was a surprising lack of other activity in the area.

The self-luminous eyes of the Dover Demon encapsulate a concept mentioned by John Keel in *The Complete Guide to Mysterious Beings*. Keel wondered if the inclusion of luminosity in these cases signified paranormal entities as opposed to flesh-and-blood animals.

CASE 23

THE ANYTHING-BUT-STANDARD SANDUSKY SASQUATCH

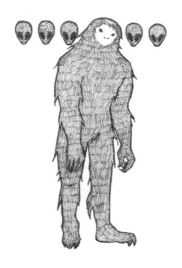

Awareness Magazine's Spring 1978 edition hailed this next sighting as "the now standard Sasquatch or Bigfoot creature", but what followed is anything but protocol even in the realms of the super-weird.

Millard Faber of Sandusky, Ohio, was an interior decorator whose side gig was to sell moss and algae to local fish stores. Around 1:30 in the afternoon of Monday, November 7 of 1977, he was hiking in a densely wooded area near Monroeville on the west branch of the Huron River, hunting for exactly that – moss and algae – when he found something entirely different.

Standing in the dense undergrowth was an eight-foot-tall, hair-covered creature with abnormally long arms. Faber described its posture as hunched and stated that it appeared to have no neck. It was entirely covered in dark hair aside from its leathery face. Set in the "normal facial position" were two orange, glowing eyes. The creature stood motionless for a moment, then jumped into the nearby river and vanished.

Faber had the presence of mind to search the area for evidence of what he had just seen. Unfortunately for Faber, one of the first pieces of evidence to assail him was a wretched odor. Pressing through the putrid stench, he uncovered huge footprints, about twenty-four inches long by eighteen inches wide, a branch with a large claw mark on it, and a seven-by-ten-foot clearing in the grass that appeared to have been made by something stomping down the plants. Faber did what he considered to be the reasonable thing and called the sheriff departments and newspapers from both adjoining counties, as his encounter had occurred on the Erie-Huron County line.

Although this sighting has so far correlated to many

truly "standard" Sasquatch encounters, it takes an abrupt turn into the realm of the highly strange.

Faber was soon joined by a deputy from both the Erie and Huron Counties Sheriff Departments, and a staff reporter from both the Erie County's *Sandusky Register* and Huron County's *Reflector-Herald*. Upon arriving to the scene, all present could still smell the terrible odor, with the exception of Huron County's Captain Larry Silcox. It may come as no surprise, either, that Captain Silcox's opinion was that the clearing had been created by pot-smokers, and then took it upon himself to pull down the claw-marked branch.

It was at this point that Faber began to suspect that a cover-up was occurring and opted not to show the party the footprint he had uncovered. As they continued on through the area, they found that the source of the water was in a hillside through some very thick undergrowth, and that around this area the odor was absolutely unbearable. Citing a lack of evidence, the decision was made not to investigate further.

According to *Awareness Magazine*, the *Sandusky Register* did publish a scant, photoless article detailing the investigation. However, it would appear that unofficial official interest in this case certainly continued.

The primary investigator of this case was a resident of the Huron, Ohio, area named Vera Perry. Not only did she write the *Awareness Magazine* article, first published in another publication, the *Eden Bulletin*, but she was also a longtime experiencer of odd phenomena in the area, including vortexes of light and a visitation by what she described as a "mushroom man". She reported that the day after the *Sandusky Register* released their article, six helicopters were spotted flying near the area of the sighting. Two days later, four more helicopters were observed in the same location. Friends of Faber would also later state that they had been chased away from the location by deputies from both the Erie and Huron Counties Sheriff's Departments. So much for giving up the investigation due to lack of evidence.

A quick note – although the words "government cover-up" are by and large more synonymous with the UFO side of the unexplained, very similar experiences are reported by those with cryptid encounters. However, unless the feds employ luminous, pink phantoms, this next leg of the case is a different type of strange entirely.

Three days after his Bigfoot encounter, Faber had retired to bed for the evening when he became aware of a presence in his room. His attention was drawn to his door, where he claimed to see five pink, glowing humanoids gliding through the air and heading in his direction. He said that each entity stood around five feet tall, had a bulbous large head, and glowing eyes. They were clad in skin-diving suits complete with a belt and walked with a pronounced stoop.

One of the strangest details of this already strange occurrence has to be their mode of travel – although they glided towards him, Faber claimed that their legs were still moving as though they were walking.

As Faber watched, the five beings filed into his room. Four of them took a seat in four chairs, which were arranged near his bed, while the fifth entity moved to about a foot by his bedside. Faber was immediately impressed by the notion that these entities were angry at him for going public with his Bigfoot sighting, claiming that he felt hatred and rage emanating from them. He also felt that they were going to take him back with them – wherever, exactly, they came from.

Faber leapt to the only defense he had and turned on a lamp. Unfortunately for him, the five angry entities remained. It was at this point that he turned to a tried-and-true method – he began yelling and swearing at the entities to get out, and exactly as in the Trasco encounter, that's precisely what they did.

However, Faber would experience similar negative feelings upon returning to the site of his Sasquatch sighting. Through the course of December 1977, Perry was in contact with both Millard Faber and his brother Robert and encouraged them to return to the area of his initial sighting. One afternoon, Robert informed Perry that they had driven to the area and stopped near a bridge that spanned a small stream. After moseying around for about three minutes in relative peace and tranquility, both brothers were immediately struck with intense anxiety. They raced out of the area and admitted later that they had both independently felt as though they were being watched.

Several of Millard's friends had reported that they had

separately driven out to the site to take a look around, only to be warned off by none other than deputies from the Erie and Huron Counties Sheriff's Departments. When Millard went to check, he too was ordered away from the area.

As odd as all of this is, Faber's experiences didn't happen in a vacuum. On November 25, at the height of her investigation into this matter, Perry's house was assailed by loud banging noises, which aroused the attention of one of her dogs. A nearly inexplicable sort of light anomaly she compared to a blue stream splashing against rocks or a whirlpool invaded her kitchen through the back door before it vanished back through the door.

One of the most poignant aspects to both his initial Sasquatch sighting and the following humanoid sighting is the prevalence of luminosity in both cases. The Sasquatch, spotted during daylight, had glowing orange eyes. The humanoids were themselves a glowing pink, also with glowing eyes. Considering the similar shape of both the luminous humanoids and the Sasquatch, along with the telepathic impression given to Faber, it seems reasonable to suggest that, not only were these apparently different types of entities tied, but that maybe they were from the same source.

The instance of telepathy that Faber described is common enough in cryptid encounters. Many witnesses claim that they feel the creature is angry at being spotted or exudes an aura of menace as though to warn them from mentioning their sighting. In this case, however, the bedroom invaders seemed to convey the sort of warning that is usually associated with cryptids at the time of the sighting. Of course, such warnings are not restricted to vague impressions from glowing pink humanoids or the eyes of a dogman. The ominous Men in Black, typically of ufological fame, have at times shown up after cryptid encounters as well.

Regarding the humanoids' mode of travel: this action of "walking on air", similar to "treading water" or "swimming", has been ascribed to many different UFO-related entities, including a very intriguing case from the *Northern UFO News, No. 82*. In Baddeley Green, Staffordshire, in the autumn of 1976, a young boy reporting seeing small beings "swimming" through the air. However, Faber's particular description of the beings "walking" through the air also falls squarely in one of the paranormal field's other categories – ghosts and hauntings. Numerous sightings of ghosts claim that they appear to walk either above or in the floors, and it's claimed that this is due to the fact that as times change so too do floor levels, and that the dead simply can't keep up with renovations.

However, this same behavior is seen exhibited in this case with nary a haunting in sight. It's intriguing that, regardless of the decidedly unconventional humanoids, they exhibit a behavior classically tied to spirits of the departed, further evidence that the same actions are enacted by apparently separate types of paranormal phenomena.

A final note must be said on the clothing of Faber's

entities. The description of some skintight "diving suit" is a style seen on countless UFO-related entities, typically with the inclusion of one accessory – a belt. According to Cutchin and Renner's *Where the Footprints End*, this is also one of the most common items of clothing observed in Sasquatch encounters. Citing Montague Summers's book *The Werewolf*, they draw the connection between these accounts of belted Bigfoots and the enchanted girdles associated with werewolf transformation and magical practice.

In this regard, looking at the belt as a symbol of transformation, particularly of the hirsute variety, brings up an intriguing point – is there a true division between the Bigfoot-like creature and the glowing humanoids? Luminosity is a factor in both accounts – the Sasquatch was said to have glowing, orange eyes, while the entities claimed both glowing eyes and were themselves glowing pink, a mere step away on the color spectrum. Too, the Sasquatch was observed to walk with a stoop, while the entities were also observed to walk with a stoop.

While this may not be the question of "is Bigfoot a spaceman in a suit?", it is certainly a question of what, exactly, are we looking at? The ties in silhouette, as well as the connection felt by Faber to exist between the Bigfoot and the humanoids, could be looked at as evidence that both apparently different types of entities were one and the same, translated by the expectations of Faber – or perhaps more appropriately, the expectations of Faber's culture and subconscious – to be a giant ape-man in the woods, and bizarre humanoids in his home.

Faber's experience also occurred at the boundary between two counties, yet another example of a liminal point. As discussed in different sections throughout this book, liminality seems to be one of the defining aspects of paranormal encounters – things that are not quite here, not quite there, but existing at a true crossroads of ambiguity.

SPECULATIONS

This has been a jaunt through the weirder side of our world, through the accounts of people who have claimed contact with things far outside of the ordinary. The question remains; just what have these people experienced?

To recap, we've had pancake-slinging flying saucer occupants, luminous-eyed Bigfoots on more than one occasion, a similar luminous-eyed Bigfoot followed by glowing pink humanoids, a clown-like automaton, Frogmen and robots and spaceships (oh my), plus many more.

As much high strangeness as is packed into this volume, this is hardly the tip of the iceberg – it's more like one snowflake in the Himalayas. When facing the vast scope of unexplained phenomena, where do we start?

PATTERNS BETWIXT AND BETWEEN

One of the most prevalent aspects across each apparently separate branch of paranormal phenomena is the presence of light anomalies in encounters. The sighting of the Flight Suit Entity is one of the most dramatic of these cases and included not just orbs of light, but a humanoid-shaped light as well. Similarly, so-called UFO-related entities are sometimes merely accompanied by a strange light, thought to be a craft of some sort only in the framework of our current culture and some stretch of the imagination. Trasco's luminous, egg-shaped object and the egg-shaped object of the Winsted Encounter definitely illuminate this concept. And hairy hominids such as Momo and Roro have been seen in conjunction with luminous phenomena.

Light also makes an appearance with the entities themselves, showing up as luminous eyes or aspects of clothing; this concept will be covered a few pages on.

One of the strangest aspects regarding light anomalies, however, is how often they seem to serve as the catalyst for an encounter. The same can be said of anomalous noises. Time and again, an encounter with a strange being is preceded by a noise – like the disembodied voice heard by Lou Rogers prior to the Roachdale disturbances, or the siren-like wail that preceded Sandown Sam – or a light – such as the sighting of the fireball prior to Flatwoods, or the blue light first observed by Hickson and Parker in the Pascagoula abduction.

Researchers of all sorts have commented on the importance of light across anomalous phenomena – Keel wondered whether the lights may be the only objectively true part of the experience, all other appearances serving only as distraction or mask. In his fantastic book *Daimonic Reality*, Patrick Harpur noted that many paranormal disturbances seem to have a dual form – a light, and a more hard-and-fast object or entity. Jenny Randles, noted British UFO researcher, also found that repeater witnesses often had early sightings of light anomalies when they were young.

On the topic of so-called repeaters, that is also a major piece of evidence for the notion that every apparently separate branch of paranormal research is actually part of the same darn tree. Witnesses to one type of anomaly will often find themselves, or their families, beset by others. One of the most immediate examples of this was the case of Faber's "standard" Sasquatch encounter – which was then followed by a quintet of floating, glowing humanoids. Mr. Y claimed a series of UFO encounters prior to his daughter's sighting of the bizarre, berry-picking, clown-like creature that called itself "Sam". And the ambiguous case of transportation that occurred to the two Nodolf children in the 1880s is said to have ushered in nightly poltergeist manifestations that continue, according to local legend, to this very day.

Electronic interference or electromagnetic distur-bances have long been associated with the paranormal, specifically the fields of spectrology and ufology. It's an adage of ghosthunters to "bring extra batteries", as batteries in electronic devices are said to drain in the presence of ghostly activity. Too, electromagnetic field disturbances are so widely associated with ghosts as to earn EMF detectors a perennial spot in any ghost-hunter's toolkit. UFO-related electronic interference and vehicular failure are also widely reported and widely accepted.

What can be made of the Marlinton Encounter? In this case, the witness's vehicle failed as, simultaneously, a Sasquatch-like creature was observed. Although this may seem like a once-in-a-lifetime chance, said sighting and attendant vehicle failure happened again mere miles down the road. Radio interference was also cited at the same moment Wetzel saw his leaf-scaled Lizardman, and the four teens who encountered the pouch-covered Flight Suit Creature claimed that their car refused to start at first as they tried to flee the scene. This was also claimed by Calvin Parker of the infamous Pascagoula abduction, which, even for its inclusion among the classic cases of ufology, was termed by none other than J. Allen Hynek to reflect religious experiences.

The description of anomalous beings as looking "off" also warrants discussion. "Off" can mean a lot of things, and true, we are talking about entities whose very appearance is unexpected. However, the use of such terms as "wrong", "funny-looking" and "disproportionate" dominate entity accounts and seem to add an additional sense of unreality to the creature observed. At Sharpsville, primary witness Dale King claimed that the beast's helmetlike head didn't look apelike or humanlike and appeared "wrong" atop its body. Hunnicutt's gnomen were markedly lopsided. And in the case of the Winsted Connecticut

Creatures, one of the reporting witnesses believed that one appeared "clearer" than the other.

WALKING PARADOXES

One of the prominent aspects across many of these accounts is the paradoxical nature of these experiences. In keeping up with all the disclosure talk earlier in 2021, something that consistently stood out to me (okay, if I'm being honest here, it drove me up the wall) was the insistence that the phenomenon discussed was a "physical" phenomenon.

I don't disagree with that statement. It's obvious that paranormal disturbances, whether ghosts, UFOs, or cryptids, oftentimes have physical effects on the environment or the witness. So, yes, therefore the phenomenon must be physical.

However – and this is a big however – *the same disturbances often exhibit nonphysical abilities.* A prime example of this is the Roachdale Creature. To suit the claims, it had to be physical – it flattened a fence, killed about 170 chickens, and beat on the walls of the Rogers family home.

In addition to these physical effects, it also was capable of appearing translucent. Bullets seemed to have no effect. It left no tracks in the mud through which it walked. To suit *those* claims, it must have been immaterial.

In our current culture, we often think of things in

terms of this or that, yes or no, paper or plastic. Many para-normal experiences seem to exist at a sort of phenomeno-logical crossroads or, to use a popular term from the far side of paranormal research, a liminal point between physi-cality and immateriality.

One of the great arguments of paranormal research is that the events may be hallucinatory in nature. I will say that many cases exhibit a dreamlike quality, populated with beings that don't abide by purely physical laws, rife with faulty transitions and nonsensical – typically on second glance, symbolic – details. However, the problem with this theory lies again in that paradox. Not only are physical traces often left, or physical effects often enacted, but objective confirmation of the event is common.

One of the greatest confirmations is the behavior of animals in conjunction with a sighting. Numerous accounts throughout this book – Kelly-Hopkinsville, Sharpsville, and Trasco, to name a few – actually begin with the witnesses being alerted to the event by their dogs. Other events, such as Cussac and Flatwoods, showcase animal response to an anomaly once the encounter is underway.

Beyond animal response, we often see that anomalous events have multiple witnesses, usually in different spheres of contact or observation. At Cussac, while no other witness to the strange beings came forward, a nearby farmer reportedly heard the same whistling noise reported by the children. The Loveland Heights case is of note here and exhibits both animal response and human confirmation.

The Magnones were awakened by the barking of their dog and noticed a putrid odor. Nearby, their neighbor was also awakened by the dog and, looking out the window, saw a strange, "foliage-covered" being. We're hard-pressed to determine the core of this anomaly – what came first, the creature or the stink? – but we can easily postulate that the being was connected to the odor based on countless other cases detailing similar rank odors with strange beings. The dog likely noticed the scent and quite possibly the small being as well. Beyond that fact, both the Magnones and the unnamed neighbor lady witnessed something odd at the same time.

These confirmation aspects of anomalous events lend a reality to them, and an objectivity. We can no longer place these events in the purely subjective or hallucinatory bin.

LOST IN TRANSMOGRIFICATION?

It's no secret I'm a major fan of investigator and author John Keel. His handling of the paranormal was with a deft blend of respect and humor that is something any student of high strangeness aspires to have. Too, his originality in dealing with the unexplained yielded several concepts that have definitely influenced the way I look at these accounts.

The first is the concept of the superspectrum, the

notion that anomalous beings may not call this neck of the woods home but, rather, have their source outside of the visible range of the electromagnetic spectrum. This is a tidy explanation for some of the peskier issues associated with paranormal phenomena, such as the annoying tendency for such things as hairy monsters and flying saucers to appear and disappear at will.

Carrying along this line of reasoning, and in particular as it pertains to seemingly physical entities that show up, traipse around, and then vanish, Keel referred to these beings as "transmogrifications of energy", envisioning a temporary form that somehow manifests on this side of the spectrum for only a time, causing varying degrees of damage or disturbance.

In a similar vein, Paul Devereux in his book *Earth Lights* discussed the concept he termed "proto-entities". Following the concept that, oftentimes, entities associated with UFOs retain some material tie to their "craft" – such as being comprised of the same material as the associated object (as in the case of the luminous being and orbs in the Flight Suit Entity Case), holding onto an object comprised of the same material (the thermos of the Simonton Encounter), or having some element of their outfit reflect the object (the buttons on Trasco's space leprechaun). He theorized that this is due to the fact that both the "craft" and the "entity" are actually comprised of the same malleable energy, an energy that has some rapport with the mind of the witness.

This concept of similitude between apparently

different objects or entities would explain the strange "acting as one" concept that pops up from time to time in encounters – namely the graceful, simultaneous motion of Hunnicutt's gnomen and the simultaneous response of Shrum's humanoids, robots, and mothership to fire.

The malleable nature of both the proto-entity concept and Keel's transmogrification of energy theory would also help explain the sheer number of different types of manifestations, something that the nuts-and-bolts, flesh-and-blood concepts have so far failed to do.

Too, I find the notion of something manifesting – or transmogrifying – in this slice of the spectrum to neatly fit such malformed monstrosities as the Enfield Horror or the Flight Suit Creature. Along a similar line of reasoning, faceless entities may be explained as things that, for one reason or another, are not totally formed.

Harkening back to an important concept, I find it intriguing that a good number of occurrences – not all, but a good number – detail anomalous lights or sounds as the first occurrence, as though these vaguer anomalies usher in the more hard-and-fast sightings of, say, a spaceman. It is as though Devereux suggests – there is a "hardening" of the malleable energy into a specific form. The question remains; are these lights and noises somehow priming the witness, or are they an effect of the entity manifesting? Or are both these concepts somehow one and the same?

It seems to me, in light of countless accounts of and theories regarding paranormal phenomena, that the hard-and-fast encounters of different creatures and craft are not the core of the phenomenon, but rather act as a kaleido-scopic lens for, as Keel termed it, "the string", the real center of these manifestations.

That's not to say the image is worthless – far from it, and the symbolic importance will be discussed in the next few pages – just that it is not solely what we perceive it or believe it to be. In these encounters, I believe that the image exists at a liminal point between objective reality and subjective experience, which, like every great mask, serves as both disguise and revelation.

SYMBOLS

Numerous researchers have picked up on the symbolic overtones of entity encounters, relating to analytical psychology, religions, and folklore worldwide. The Fairy Faith of the British Isles is one of the most oft-referenced of folkloric traditions in relation to modern encounters, and with good reason; many of the tropes see themselves repre-sented in modern lore. We have pinned down the simi-larity of Simonton's pancakes to the buckwheat cakes of the Good Folk, and the green powder of Trasco's encounter to the association of fairies with dust. However, I believe that these symbols run even deeper than our cultural recollections of folklore and are reminiscent of archetypal experiences, stemming from the collective unconscious envisioned by none other than Carl Jung.

Jung himself commented on the relation of the image of the flying saucer to the mandala in his work *Flying Saucers: A Modern Myth of Things Seen in the Sky*. If we take a symbolic look at many paranormal encounters, the appearance of the entity or object in question ties into such archetypal motifs, such as the egg-shaped craft analogous with the Cosmic Egg, or Sasquatch to the Wild Man.

I find it intriguing as well that even beliefs regarding the paranormal have their counterpart in folklore and symbolism. Modern researchers suggest that waterways and cave systems are two of the ingredients in the mystery soup that make up paranormal hotspots. Not only do these two aspects correlate with traditional beliefs regarding the common roost for denizens of the otherworld, as well as portals to said otherworld, across cultures worldwide, but they also have immense importance in the realm of psychological symbolism.

As mentioned previously, water is one of the most common symbols for the unconscious mind – so, too, is the cave, or subterranean world. From modern beliefs of secret subterranean alien bases to water somehow generating haunting-type phenomena, is this symbolically linked to a hidden understanding that paranormal manifestations are, at least partly, linked to the collective unconscious?

There's no denying the dreamlike nature of many paranormal occurrences. One of the most troublesome qualities when attempting to explain these manifestations is the abruptness with which these events often occur – as observed in the Winterfold Wonder, the bell-shaped, faceless thing was just there one moment, gone the next. Too, there is the magical disappearing landing gear of the Cussac sphere. Whatever the source of these manifestations truly is, it can't simply be physical – though these experiences play out in the physical plane, interacting with objects, people, and animals.

Yes – this is pure speculation. Even the collective unconscious is just one of many theories regarding the real puzzle of the human mind. And I want to be clear – in saying that these events may be linked to psychological symbolism or in referring to them as dreamlike, I'm in no way writing off these events as purely psychological or hallucinatory in nature. Both the objective confirmation of encounters and trace evidence point against that notion. However, the inclusion of such strong symbols, so deeply rooted in cultures worldwide, argues that there is at least some effect, some give-and-take, between the observer and the observed.

CROSSROADS BLUES

If the appearance of paranormal entities serves as a mask or filter for the source of the phenomenon, the question remains – what is the source, and what determines the image?

If such questions could be answered definitively, we'd have to change the name of the field to *the explained*. The difficulty in such a question is that each leg of it relies on the other. If we could identify the source, we could likely identify its mechanism, and vice versa.

Since, in the concept I've postulated, the source is hidden behind or within the image, it seems most practical to look to the image first, not relying on it as the absolute truth of the encounter, but as *a* truth of the encounter.

The varied appearances of creatures seem to be evidence of subjective influence. John Keel once postulated the concept that paranormal manifestations are reflective in nature – and, as if on cue, the phenomenon appeared to respond. In his work *The Eighth Tower*, a remarkable event appears to lend credence to this idea. Keel noted that he had been playing around with an admittedly out-there concept – that the parahumans may be aquatic. He based this half-notion on the sci-fi concept that these odd folks are often observed wearing turtlenecks – maybe, just maybe, this choice in clothing hid something like gills.

"Naturally," Keel wrote, "I didn't discuss this preposterous theory with anyone."

However, later that week, he received a letter from a young man who had been hitchhiking in Florida. The car that picked him up was not driven by a serial killer, as the urban legends might suggest – rather, it was driven by a man with gill-like flaps on his neck.

This concept of some reflective ability on the part of the phenomenon casts an added paranoia onto the paranormal that puts Fox Mulder's mental state to shame.

Imagine trying to study something that can go out of its way to confirm you're on the right track – where's the truth now?

However, this reflective ability doesn't seem to be solely responsible for the images and attributes of paranormal experiences – unless that's what "it" wants you to think...

Sarcasm aside, if the images of paranormal phenomena were solely based in the expectations of the witness, we could expect things to make a bit more sense. We would expect them to be a bit more, well, expectable. Instead, it seems as though these occurrences confirm and challenge beliefs in equal measure. Take, for example, the Flatwoods Encounter.

While the initial sighting of the eyes was assumed to be something mundane, such as a raccoon, the overall scope of the encounter falls squarely into midcentury iconography. Ronald Shaver proposed the concept of the "crashed saucer", and what entity do they contact but something straight out of a sci-fi double feature?

On the flipside, Millard Faber saw Bigfoot. The story could be as simple as that – except for the fact that he claimed glowing humanoids invaded his bedroom three nights later. The iconography of this two-part case seems in conflict with itself; why should someone expect to see such strange entities directly after seeing, for all intents and purposes, a mysterious primate?

Too, the immediacy of many encounters – such as the appearance of the Winterfold Wonder at precisely the time Freeman decided to stop his vehicle – is either one heck of a coincidence, or evidence that the encounter is resolutely linked to the observation of the witness.

Yet again, we have another liminal point, a crossroads of sorts. It seems as though the phenomenon is reflective of certain beliefs, while maintaining, as it were, a mind of its own. This phenomenon seems capable of conforming to certain beliefs, while also serving as the cause of different beliefs. In looking to the worth of these disturbances – whether in the symbolic, subjective truth of experience or the material, objective fact of occurrence – I believe the worth is somewhere at the center.

MORE THAN ONE RIGHT ANSWER

As big a fan I am of the decidedly unconventional superspectrum idea, it is also my conviction that there is room enough in this universe for multiple answers to be correct. A great example of this is Bigfoot. As referenced across the several hairy hominid cases I've included here, Sasquatch lore contains definite high-strangeness elements far more often than one might suspect. Joshua Cutchin and Timothy Renner have done a fantastic job of cataloguing these oddities in their series of two books, *Where the Footprints End*, volumes 1 and 2. That being said, I remain open to the possibility that a population of some undiscovered large primate may indeed inhabit North America.

I'm sure a handful of you are saying, "Now hold on just a footprint-casting minute – we just heard your arguments to the contrary? You mean to tell me that you think there are (for lack of a better word) spectral *and* flesh-and-blood Sasquatches?"

In a word, yes.

...or, rather, there could be. You'd be hard-pressed to find a researcher deny the existence of black dogs when faced with accounts of the Black Shuck, or the existence of women wearing white due to the ghostly Woman in White. Just because a significant number of sightings appear to correlate to a symbolic, decidedly unconventional way of looking at the phenomenon doesn't negate the fact that other answers may also be correct.

THE INCONCLUSIVE CONCLUSION

There is a question that, I suspect, every paranormal researcher is asked at some point. I have certainly been at the receiving end of this question many times, whether guesting on a podcast, through comments on my channel, or in private messages. It is a paranormal Mad Libs of sorts and runs something like this:

- Why did (fill in the anomaly) happen in (location) in (date)?
- Why did (the Momo scare) happen in (Louisiana, Missouri) in (1972)?
- Why did (the Simonton Encounter) happen in (Eagle River, Wisconsin) in (1961)?
- Why did...and so on and so forth. The unsatisfactory and short answer is that no one knows. The still-unsatisfactory, yet longer answer involves theories regarding waterways,

> ley-lines, geomagnetism, the psychic ability of
> witnesses, the prevalence of caves in the area,
> the makeup of the soil, tragedies that have
> occurred there, sunspot cycles...and circles
> back to that short admission, no one knows.

At the end of the day, that, to me, is the true importance of paranormal research. It is an admission of not knowing. The definitions we put on things have to do with their mystery: ufology, the study of *unidentified* flying objects; cryptozoology, the study of *hidden* animals. Even the broad label of this field is simply *the unexplained.*

That isn't to say that we should just throw our hands up and say, "Well, there you have it. Unknown and unexplained; everyone, go back to your homes. It's not that there's nothing to see here – it's just that we don't know what it is and probably never will."

In my opinion, it's quite the opposite.

Conventional paranormal research places much importance on proof – a crashed saucer, the definitive Sasquatch DNA, catalogued contact with a spirit. Such proof seems to always scoot out of reach, like the fruit tree of Tantalus. It is my current conviction – maybe a dead extraterrestrial will turn up tomorrow and I'll change my tune – that the proof may not be the real worth of paranormal research. If proof is not the worth of it, the question remains; what is?

There is one case I received many years ago that always sticks with me. It was not a dramatic account –

there was no missing time, no sighting of a bulletproof Bigfoot, no flashbacks or bad dreams. It was a simple, short-lived sighting of a strange thing in the sky; it didn't correlate to known craft, its behavior was unlike a weather balloon or drone. And, for the record, there was no swamp nearby. It was unexplained, sure, but there was nothing frightening or threatening about it.

However, when I finished taking the account and gave my typical sign-off – do you have any other questions? – I was not prepared for what the witness would say.

The witness in question was a no-nonsense gent from southwestern Wisconsin, part of the very demographic I had grown up with. I asked my question, and he paused. Eventually he said, "What was it?"

That question is what returns to me every time I face the concept that the unknown may be the unknowable and debate the wisdom of setting out across this vast, dark, incomprehensible sea armed only with a flashlight and some questions. The paramount importance of this field is evident in that witness's one simple question. The man was not some UFO enthusiast and claimed no previous sightings. He led a normal life in every sense of the term and wished to remain anonymous to protect that normal life, even though his sighting was, by no stretch of the imagination, wildly unbelievable – just unexplainable. He came forward simply because he had seen *something* he couldn't identify and was looking for an explanation.

In that moment, I realized I didn't have one.

To study the paranormal is to admit that we, as a

species, live alongside some great unknown. Yes, there are countless theories (including mine, I might add) regarding it, its source, its possible meaning or motives. But it remains a mystery that reaches out and grabs unsuspecting bystanders, harassing them with lights, creatures, shadows, thumps, and pancakes. True, some people who come forward enjoy the attention their report garners; others devote their lives to the mystery that they briefly glanced. However, for every witness who takes something away from their experience, there is another witness who had something taken away from them – whether that's a sense of security, a few weeks of work, or respectability. And of course, for every witness who comes forward with their account, there are ten others who never will.

The paranormal – the unexplained, the supernatural, the unknown, whatever you call it – is an important part of the human condition. And I suspect that, for all our searching, one day it may be uncovered that the truth is not only "out there", but also within ourselves.

WORKS CITED

CASE 1: THAT STRANGE NIGHT

"1881: A Possible Abduction in Southern Wisconsin." *UFOupdateslist.com,* http://ufoupdateslist.com/2000/jul/m20-020.shtml. Accessed 10 Nov. 2021.

Cornell, A. D. and Gauld, Alan. *Poltergeists, Second Edition.* Hove, White Crow Books, 2017.

Gard, Robert E. and Sorden, L. G. *Wisconsin Lore, 12*th *Printing.* Ashland, WI, Heartland Press, 1987.

"History." *Platteville.org,* https://www.platteville.org/community/page/history, Accessed 10 Nov. 2021.

"House Haunted in 1830s Still Stands Near Mound." *Platteville Journal* [Platteville, WI], undated clipping. From the collection of Roll, Todd.

"Letter to the editor: Minnie Was My Mother." *Platteville Journal* [Platteville, WI], undated clipping. From the collection of Roll, Todd.

Paulides, David. "Missing Persons May Be Tied to UFO Cases." *MUFON UFO Journal 546*, pp. 1, 7–9.

Potter, Nettie. "The Nodolf Nightmare." *Driftlessroadtrip.com*, https://driftlessroadtrip.com/the-nodolf-nightmare/. Accessed 10 Nov. 2021.

Prestegard, Steve. "Suggestion: Dont read this story alone in the dark: A tour of allegedly haunted places." *Swnews4u.com*, https://www.swnews4u.com/local/suggestion-dont-read-this-story-alone-in-the-dark/.

Roll, Todd. Personal conversation with author.

Wentz, W.Y. Evans. *The Fairy-Faith in Celtic Countries,* London, H. Frowde, 1911.

WHS Library-Archives Staff. "Platteville, Wisconsin – A Brief History." *Wisconsinhistory.org*, 2009, https://www.wisconsinhistory.org/Records/Article/CS2434, Accessed 10 Nov. 2021.

CASE 2: THE FLATWOODS MONSTER

"Braxton County Residents Report Giant Red Monster." Hinton Daily News, [Hinton, WV], 15 Sept. 1952, p. 1.

Coleman, Loren. *Mothman and Other Curious Encounters*. New York, Paraview, 2002.

"Fire-Breathing Monster." *The News and Observer* [Raleigh, NC], morning edition, 15 Sept. 1952, p. 2.

The Flatwoods Monster: A Legacy of Fear. Directed by Breedlove, Seth, Performance by May, Ed and May, Fred. Small Town Monsters, 2018.

Keel, John. *The Eighth Tower: On Ultraterrestrials and the Superspectrum,* 2nd *Edition*. San Antonio, Anomalist Books, 2013.

Sanderson, Ivan T. *Uninvited Visitors: A biologist looks at UFO's*. New York, Cowles Education Corporation, 1967.

"Seven Stick to Their Story of Seeing, Smelling Monster." The Lexington Herald [Lexington, KY], morning edition, 15 Sept 1952, p. 5.

"Story of 'Monster' in W. VA. Hills Divides Braxton County Citizenship." Brownwood Bulletin [Brownwood, TX], 15 Sept. 1952, p. 8.

CASE 3: THE LOVELAND FROGMEN

Bloecher, Ted and Davis, Isabel. *Close Encounter at Kelly and Others of 1955*. Evanston, IL, Center for UFO Studies, 1978.

Cutchin, Joshua. *The Brimstone Deceit: An In-Depth Examination of Supernatural Scents, Otherworldly Odors, and Monstrous Miasmas*. San Antonio, Anomalist Books, 2016.

Gerhard, Ken. *A Menagerie of Mysterious Beasts: Encounters with Cryptid Creatures*. Woodbury, MN, Llewellyn Publications, 2016.

Keel, John. *The Mothman Prophecies, 2nd Edition*. New York, Tor, 1991.

Renner, James. *It Came from Ohio...True Tales of the Weird, Wild, and Unexplained*. Gray and Company Publishers, 2012.

Vallee, Jacques. *Passport to Magonia: From Folklore to Flying Saucers, 2nd Edition*. Brisbane, Daily Grail Publishing, 2014.

Case 4: The Kelly Little Silver Men or the Hopkinsville Hobgoblins

"Archives: Story of space-ship, 12 little men probed today." Kentuckynewera.com, x https://www.kentuckynewera. com/eclipse/article_fecf69ce-8611-11e7-beaf-0ffce93df895.html, 20 Aug. 2017. Original article 22 Aug. 1955.

Bloecher & Davis, 1978.

Coleman, Loren. *Mysterious America*. Winchester, MA, Faber & Faber, 1983.

Keel, 2013.

Case 5: John Trasco Meets the Space Leprechaun

Gross, Loren E. *The Fifth Horseman of the Apocalypse: UFOs, A History*. Fremont, CA, 1997.

Keel, John. "Cattle Rustling in the 20th Century, Strange Things are Happening to Animals." *The Daily Times-News* [Burlington, NC] 31 Oct. 1967, p. A13.

Keel, John. *The Complete Guide to Mysterious Beings, 3rd Edition*. New York, Tor, 2002.

Moore, Ken. "Incidents Recalled." The Courier-News [Bridgewater, NJ] 31 Mar. 1967, p. 13.

Rhys, John. *Celtic Folklore: Welsh and Manx, Volume 1 of 2.* Oxford, Clarendon Press, 1901. Vallee, 2014. Wentz, 1911.

Case 6: Wetzel's Riverside Weirdo

Bitto, Robert. "Xoloitzcuintli: Sacred Dog of the Ancient Mexicans." *Mexicounexplained.com,* http://mexicounexplained.com/xoloitzcuintli-sacred-dog-of-the-ancient-mexicans/. Accessed 10 Mar. 2021.

Briggs, Katharine. *An Encyclopedia of Faires, Hobgoblins, Browines, Bogies, and Other Supernatural Creatures.* New York, Pantheon, 1976.

Bunn, Ivan. "Black Dogs & Water." *Fortean Times, no. 17, August 1976,* pp. 12–13.

Coleman, 1983.

Conway, Moncure Daniel. *Demonology and Devil-Lore.* New York, Henry Holt and Company, 1879.

Johnson, Patrick. "Count Dracula and the Folkloric Vampire: Thirteen Comparisons," *Journal of Dracula Studies: Vol. 3 , Article 6.*

Jung, C. G. *Collected Works of C. G. Jung, Volume 9 (Part 1): Archetypes and the Collective Unconscious.* Princeton, NJ, Princeton University Press, 2014.

Keel, 2002.

"One of Those Hallowe'en Things Comes to Life." *The Sacramento Bee* [Sacramento, CA], 10 Nov. 1958, p. B7.

"Riverside Police Suffer from 'Monster' Fatigue." *The Coulton Courier* [Coulton, CA], 11 Nov. 1958, p. 1.

"Sober Driver Reports Monster." *Oroville Mercury Register* [Oroville, CA], 10 Nov. 1958, p. 5.

"Unidentified Flying Monster? Abominable Noman Rides Again Along Santa Ana River Bottom." *The San Bernardino County Sun* [San Bernardino, CA], 11 Nov. 1958, pp. B1, B5.

Winick, Stephen. "Introducing the Green Man." *Blogs.loc.gov,* 15 Jan. 2021. https://blogs.loc.gov/folklife/2021/01/introducing-the-green-man/, accessed 10 Nov. 2021.

CASE 7: FLIX, THE CREATURE THAT MADE A NAME FOR ITSELF

"14 Feet Tall, Walks Upright: Hairy 'Monster' Seen in

Woods at Tenmile." *The News-Review* [Roseburg, Oregon], 21 Oct. 1959, p. 1.

"Boys Warn About Shots At Monster." *Greater Oregon* [Albany, OR] 19 Aug 1960, p. 1.

Editor's Mailbag. "Wants Picture of Monster". *Greater Oregon*, [Albany, OR], 19 Aug. 1960, p. 3.

"Falsity Clings to Life." *Albany Democrat Herald* [Albany, OR], 7 Oct. 1964, p. 4.

Kinsey, Mickey. "Off the Beat", *Corvallis Gazette-Times* [Corvallis, OR], 10 Sep. 1960, pp. 1, 7.

Westby, Betty. "Don't Shoot At Mystery Monster of Conser Lake." *Greater Oregon* [Albany, OR], 12 Aug 1960, p.1.

Westby, Betty. "Interest Revives in Elusive Conser Lake Monster: Eye-Witness Refutes Radio KGW Report". *Greater Oregon*, [Albany, OR], 21 Oct. 1960, p. 1.

CASE 8: THE MARLINTON ENCOUNTER

"Braxton Monstor (sic) 'Branching Out'." *Hinton Daily News* [Hinton, WV] 5 Jan. 1961, p. 8.

"Braxton Monster Reportedly Seen by Truck Driver." *Beckley Post-Herald/The Raleigh Register* [Beckley, WV], 1 Jan. 1961, p. 5.

Keel, 2002.

"For People in Marion County Monster Stories Aren't So Funny." *The Weirton Daily Times* [Weirton, West Virginia], 08 Aug. 1961, p. 3.

"New Sightings Reported." *The Raleigh Register* [Beckley, WV], 5 Jan. 1961, p. 1.

"Posse Finds Rocks Upturned: Is Braxton Monster Back? Truck Driver Believes So." *The Charleston Daily Mail* [Charleston, WV], 31 Dec. 1960, pp. 1, 3.

CASE 9: SIMONTON'S FAMOUS FLYING FLAPJACKS

"Aerial Study Unit Not High On Eagle River Space Cake." *Green Bay Press-Gazette* [Green Bay, WI], 3, May 1961, p. 1.

Allen, John F. "Flapjack Fancies? Flying Saucer Folk Defiant." *The San Francisco Examiner,* 5 Mar. 1962, p. 4.

"Claims He Swapped Water, Cookies With 'Spacemen.'" *The Sheboygan Press* [Sheboygan, WI], 24 Apr. 1961, p. 4.

Cutchin, Joshua. *A Trojan Feast: The Food and Drink Offerings of Aliens, Faeries, and Sasquatch.* San Antonio, Anomalist Books, 2015.

"Eagle River Plumber (With Good Reputation) Tells of Flying Saucer: Trades Jug of Water for Three Cosmic Cookies." *Chippewa Herald-Telegram* [Chippewa Falls, WI], 24 Apr. 1961, p. 1.

"Flying Saucer Lands in Vilas, Man Claims." *Wisconsin State Journal* [Madison, WI], 23 Apr. 1961, pp. 1, 2.

"Flying Saucer Crew Drops in, Shares Cakes." *Leader-Telegram* [Eau Claire, WI], 23 Apr. 1961, p. 1.

Godfrey, Linda. *The Michigan Dogman: Werewolves and Other Unknown Canines Across the U. S. A.* Eau Claire, WI, Unexplained Research Publishing Company, 2010.

Hynek, J. Allen and Vallee, Jacques. *The Edge of Reality: A progress report on Unidentified Flying Objects.* Chicago, Henry Regnery Company, 1975.

Keel, John. *Operation Trojan Horse: The Classic Breakthrough Study of UFOs, 3rd Edition.* San Antonio, Anomalist Books, 2013.

"More Folks Report Flying Saucer Sightings In State." *The Sheboygan Press* [Sheboygan, WI], 28 Apr. 1961, p. 11.

"More Tales of Saucers." *Kenosha News* [Kenosha, WI], 28 Apr. 1961, p. 20.

Sinistrari. *De delictis et poenis.* Venice, Albriccium, 1700.

Vallee, 2014.

Wentz, 1911.

CASE 10: THE THREE-RING CIRCUS OF CISCO GROVE

Clelland, Mike. *The Messengers: Owls, Synchronicity and the UFO Abductee, Second Edition.* Mike Clelland, 2020.

Lawrence, Robert Means. *The Magic of the Horse-Shoe With Other Folk-Lore Notes.* New York, Houghton, Mifflin and Company, 1898.

Lore, Gordon. *Strange Effects from UFOs: A NICAP Special Report.* Washington, The National Investigations Committee on Aerial Phenomena, 1969.

Lorenzen, Coral and Jim. *Flying Saucer Occupants.* New York, Signet, 1967.

Morris, Ian. *Death-Ritual and Social Structure in Classical Antiquity.* Cambridge, Cambridge University Press, 1992.

Torres, Noe and Uriarte, Ruben. *Aliens in the Forest :The Cisco Grove UFO Encounter.* Roswell Books, 2011.

Vallee, 2014.

CASE 11: WALL DONUTS, WATERMELON CLOUDS, AND WALKING STUMPS

Brandon, Jim. *Weird America: A Guide to Places of Mystery in the United States.* New York, E. P. Dutton, 1978.

"Coastal UFO List Said Not Impressive." *Corvallis Gazette-Times* [Corvallis, OR], 18 Oct. 1966, p. 2.

Cornell & Guald, 2017.

Keel, 2002.

Lloyd, Dan. "Crawling Lights – A New Development." *Flying Saucer Review, Vol. 13 No. 3,* May-June 1967, pp. 29-30.

"Oregon Puzzlers: Strange Things are Happening." *The Spokesman-Review* [Spokane, WA], 18 Oct. 1966, p. 2.

"Weird Aerial Phenomena In Oregon." *The A.P.R.O Bulletin,* November-December 1966, p. 6.

CASE 12: THE CASE OF THE CUSSAC DEVILS

Cutchin, 2016.

Mesnard, Joel and Pavy, Claude. "Encounter with 'Devils'." *Flying Saucer Review, Vol. 14, No. 5.* September/October 1968, pp. 7–9.

Vallee, 2014.

Wentz, 1911.

CASE 13: THE CONNECTICUT CREATURES

"INTCAT 1967 JULY-DEC". Intcat.blogspot.com. http://intcat.blogspot.com/search/label/1967%20JUL%20-%20DEC Retrieved 07/17/21.

Keel, 1991.

Lorenzen, Coral and Jim. *UFOs Over the Americas.* New York, Signet Books, 1968.

Vallee, 2014.

CASE 14: THE WEIRD WINTERFOLD WONDER

Bowen, Charles. "The Spectre of Winterfold." *Flying Saucer Review, Vol. 14, No. 1 January/February 1968*, pp. 15–16.

"Faceless Rider: Surrey Ghosts, Folklore and Forteana." *Paranormaldatabase.com,* https://www.paranormaldatabase.com/surrey/surrdata.php?pageNum_paradata=1&totalRows_paradata=141, accessed 1 Nov 2021.

Harpur, Patrick. *Daimonic Reality: A Field Guide to the Otherworld,* 2nd *Edition.* Ravensdale, WA, Pine Winds Press, 2003.

Hauck, Dennis. *Haunted Places: The National Directory.* New York, Penguin Books, 2002.

Lodge, Matthew. "The ghost that has haunted Lincoln park for 40 years: This ghostly apparition has left people terrified." *LincolnshireLive.co.uk,* https://www.lincolnshirelive.co.uk/news/lincoln-news/ghost-haunted-lincoln-park-40-3711218. Accessed 10 Jan. 2021.

Swayne, Matthew L. *Haunted Rails: Tales of Ghost Trains, Phantom Conductors, and Other Railroad Spirits.* Llewellyn Worldwide, 2019.

Vallee, 2014.

CASE 15: THE SHARPSVILLE SHAMBLER

Bord, Colin and Janet. "The UFO/Bigfoot Connection." *Flying Saucer Review, Vol.* 25, *No.* 3, September 1979, pp. 24–27.

Clark, Jerome and Coleman, Loren. *The Unidentified & Creatures of the Outer Edge, Special Edition.* San Antonio, Anomalist Books, 2006.

Cutchin, Joshua and Renner, Timothy. *Where the Footprints End: High Strangeness and the Bigfoot Phenomenon, Volume 1, Folklore.* Dark Holler Arts, 2020.

Godfrey, Linda. *Hunting the American Werewolf.* Madison, WI, Trails Books, 2006.

Worley, Don. "The UFO-Related Anthropoids – An Important New Opportunity for Investigator-Researchers with Courage." Proceedings of the 1976 CUFOS Conference, 2nd Edition, 1976, pp. 287–294.

CASE 16: THE FLIGHT SUIT ENTITY

Bord, Colin and Janet. "The UFO/Bigfoot Connection." *Flying Saucer Review, Vol.* 25, *No.* 3, September 1979, pp. 24–27.

Clark, & Coleman, 2006.

"CUFOS Report 72-01. January 19th, 1972." *CUFOS.org.* http://www.cufos.org/HUMCAT/ HUMCAT_Index_1972.pdf. Accessed 20 Mar. 2021.

"Darrell Keith Rich aka 'Young Elk'", *clarprosecutor.org,* http://www.clarkprosecutor.org/html/death/US/ rich620.htm. Accessed 20 Mar. 2021.

Devereux, Paul. *Earth Lights: Towards an Explanation of the UFO Enigma.* Wellingborough, Northamptonshire, Turnstone Press Limited, 1982.

"Multiple Witness Case in California", *The A.P.R.O. Bulletin,* March-April 1972, pp. 1, 5.

Keel, 2002.

Keel, 1991.

Lecouteux, Claude. *Demons and Spirits of the Land: Ancestral Lore and Practices (Graham, Jon, Trans.).* Rochester, Vermont, Inner Traditions, 2015.

"Rich's victims: 9 women, girls, ages 11 to 27." *Sfgate.com,* 12 Mar. 2000, https://www.sfgate.com/news/article/ Rich-s-victims-9-women-girls-ages-11-to-27-3069853.php. Accessed 20 Mar. 2021.

CASE 17: MOMO – THE MISSOURI MONSTER

Blackburn, Ken. *Momo: The Strange Case of the Missouri Monster.* LegendScape Publishing, 2019.

Coleman, 1983.

Harpur, 2003.

Hauck, 2002.

Keel, 2002.

Keel, 2013.

Keel, 1991.

Lodge, Matthew. "The ghost that has haunted Lincoln Park for 40 years: This ghostly apparition has left people terrified." LincolnshireLive.co.uk, https://www.lincolnshirelive.co.uk/news/lincoln-news/ghost-haunted-lincoln-park-40-3711218. Accessed 10 Jan. 2021.

Sanderson, 1967.

CASE 17: RORO – THE ROACHDALE CREATURE

Clark, Jerome. "On the Trail of Unidentified Furry Objects." *Greater Oregon* [Albany, OR] 13 Jul. 1973, p. 2.

Clark & Coleman, 2006.

Godfrey, Linda. *Monsters Among Us: An Exploration of Otherworldly Bigfoots, Wolfmen, Portals, Phantoms, and Odd Phenomena.* New York, Tarcher Perigree, 2016.

Randles, Jenny. *Mind Monsters: Invaders from Inner Space?* Northamptonshire, The Aquarian Press, 1990.

CASE 19: THE ENFIELD HORROR

Coleman, 1983.

"Could Enfield monster be a kangaroo?" *Southern Illinoisan* [Carbondale, Il], 16 May 1973, p. 2.

Dettro, Chris. "McDaniel and the monster of Enfield." *Daily News-Post* [Monrovia, CA] 30 Jul. 1973, pp. A1, A8.

"Enfield Monster – the beginning of a legend?" *St. Cloud Times* [Saint Cloud, MN] 7 May 1973, p. 2.

"Fail to Find Monster at Enfield, Ill." *The Terre Haute Tribune* [Terre Haute, IN], 14 May 1973, p. 3.

Lecouteux, Claude. *The Tradition of Household Spirits: Ancestral Lore and Practices.* Rochester, Vermont, Inner Traditions, 2013.

Matyi, Bob. "Enfield's Monster: It's still there whatever it is." *Evansville Courier and Press* [Evansville, IN] 8 May 1973, p. 1.

Montgomery, Dennis. "'Three Legs, Pink Eyes As Big As Flashlights': A 'Monster' At Enfield." *Mt. Vernon Register-News* [Mt. Vernon, IL] 27 Apr. 1973, p. 1.

"No Open Season On Monsters." *The Daily Reporter* [Greenfield, IN], 9 May 1973, p. 1.

CASE 20: SANDOWN SAM

Bord, Colin and Janet. *Modern Mysteries of Britain: One Hundred Years of Strange Events.* London, Diamond Books, 1991.

CUFOS. "HumCat #1201". *Cufos.org,* http://www.cufos.org/HUMCAT/HUMCAT_Index_1973.pdf , accessed 30 Jul. 2021.

Keel, 1991.

Oliver, Norman. "Report-Extra! Ghost or Spaceman '73?" *BUFORA Journal,* Volume 06, No 05, Jan/Feb 1978.

CASE 21: THE PASCAGOULA ABDUCTION

Blum, Judy and Ralph. "All They Meant to do Was Go Fishing." *Nicap.org,* *https://www.nicap.org/reports/ 731011pascagoula_hicksontape.htm* Accessed 17 April 2020.

Broom, Brian. "'The story is very true. That's what has bothered me for 45 years.' UFO Witnesses Speak." *Clarionledger.com,* https://www.clarionledger.com/story/ magnolia/2019/03/14/ufo-pascagoula-mississippi-calvin-parker-charles-hickson-other-witnesses/3129121002/.

Clark, Jerome. "Startling New Evidence in the Pascagoula and Adamski Abductions." *UFO Report, August 1978,* pp. 36–79.

Hickson, Charles and Mendez, William. *UFO Contact at Pascagoula.* CreateSpace, 1983.

Hynek & Vallee, 1975.

Keel, 2013.

Keel, 1991.

Parker, Calvin. *Pascagoula – The Closest Encounter: My Story.* Flying Disk Press, 2018.

"The Pascagoula – Mississippi's Singing River: A Mermaid in Mississippi?" *exploresouthernhistory.com*, https://www.exploresouthernhistory.com/pascagoula2

Stringfield, Leonard. *Situation Red: The UFO Siege*. New York, Doubleday & Co Inc, 1977.

"What Swims, Glows, and Chases Boats?" *Cincinnati Post*, 8 Nov. 1973 (clipping).

Wilson, Colin. *Alien Dawn: An Investigation into the Contact Experience*. Woodbury, MN, Llewyn Publications, 1998.

Webb, David. *1973 – Year of the Humanoids: An Analysis of the Fall, 1973 UFO/Humanoid Wave, Second Edition*. Evanston, IL, Center for UFO Studies, 1976.

CASE 22: THE DOVER DEMON

Clark & Coleman, 2006.

Coleman, 1983.

Connolly, Margaret. "Mysterious creatures reported in two states." *The Lowell Sun* [Lowell, MA], 16 May 1977, p. 1.

"Dover in Middle Earth?" *The Boston Globe,* 30 May 1977, p. 40.

"This monster may be a hoax, then again..." *The Boston Globe,* 16 May 1977, p. 1.

Case 23: The Anything-but-Standard Sandusky Sasquatch

Cornell, & Gauld, 2017.

Cutchin & Renner, 2020.

"Flying Entities Reported from the Midlands" *Northern UFO News No* 82, Warrington, Cheshire, 1981, pp. 5–6.

"HumCat Index 1977." Cufos.org, http://www.cufos.org/ HUMCAT/HUMCAT_Index_1977.pdf   Accessed   15 Jun. 2021.

Perry, Vera. "The Huron Visitations: A Personal Narrative." *Awareness, Spring 1978,* Vol.7 No. 1, pp. 5–17.

Rosales, Albert. Humanoid Encounters 1975–1979: The Others Amongst Us. CreateSpace, 2016.

Summers, Montague. *The Werewolf in Lore and Legend, Second Edition.* Mineola, NY, Dover Publications, 2003.

SPECULATIONS

Cutchin, Joshua and Renner, Timothy. *Where the Footprints End: High Strangeness and the Bigfoot Phenomenon, Volumes 1 & 2.* Dark Holler Arts, 2020.

Devereux, 1982.

Harpur, 2003.

Jung, C. G. *Flying Saucers: A Modern Myth of Things Seen in the Sky (Hull, R. F.C., trans.)* Princetown, New Jersey, Princeton University Press, 1979.

Keel, 2002.

Keel, 2013.

Keel, 1991.

Randles, Jenny. *The Startling Facts of the Investigation into the Pennine UFO Mystery.* London, Granada, 1983.

ABOUT THE AUTHOR

Inspired by the rich history of weirdness throughout her home state of Wisconsin, Zelia Edgar has had a lifelong interest in the paranormal and has been seriously researching it for over a decade. In that time, her interest has evolved from the conventional to the high strangeness.

You can contact Zelia at www.justanothertinfoil-hat.com.